Wellbeing

Julie Johnson

Series Editor: Emma Bartley

GRESHAM BOOKS

Published by
Gresham Books Limited
The Carriage House
Ningwood Manor
Ningwood
Isle of Wight
PO30 4NJ

Main Cover Image: Thinkstock

ISBN 978-0-946095-62-9

Design by Words & Pictures
Typesetting and layout by Fiona Jerome
Printed in the UK

Acknowledgements

This book has been the journey of a professional lifetime. It may have been penned by me, but many took part in the journey of its coming into being. I have worked with children, adolescents and their parents for the last 25 years, and it is them I wish to thank first and foremost for enabling me to write this book. Children and young people have great insight and wisdom; every day they have challenged and inspired me.

Parenting is the most wonderful, stretching, fulfilling and difficult job that those of us fortunate enough to be blessed with children ever undertake. We are reminded daily through the eyes of children to value, appreciate and savour those things in life we have so often forgotten, and my own children have done exactly that for me. I wish to thank Jamie and Amy for the part they have played in teaching me what it is to be a parent—in both the uplifting moments and the not so easy ones.

May I also thank those who have been with me on this parenting journey: those friends who have supported, inspired and challenged me as a parent, and have been part of the 'village' raising my children with myself and Peter.

May I also thank those in my professional life who have influenced me: Joe Griffin and Ivan Tyrell who developed the 'Human Givens' model of psychotherapy; Chris Cullen and Richard Burnett who started the 'Mindfulness in School Project', bringing mindfulness to children in both primary and senior school (and Chris Cullen in particular for his support and guidance as I have sought to cultivate my own mindfulness practice); the schools I have had the privilege to work with over the years, which have entrusted their pupils and parents to me; the parents who have honoured me by sharing their struggles and concerns, and allowing me to work with them and their children.

Thanks also to Nick Oulton who invited me to write this book, and Emma Bartley, my ever patient editor, who took my 20,000 excess word count and helped me make this book what it is today.

Finally thank you to Peter, my husband of many years, without whom none of this would have been possible. Thank you for your love, support and the privilege of working with you.

Julie Johnson

Wellbeing

CONTENTS

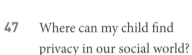

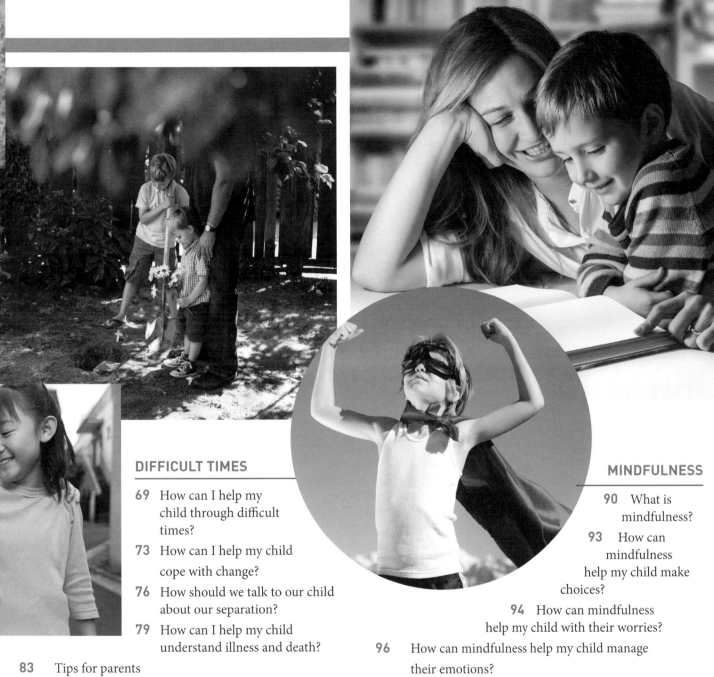

Introduction

At the turn of the century, when writing the book Counselling in Schools (together with Robert Bor), I was battling to highlight the mental health agenda and raise the profile of wellbeing in schools. Teachers weren't always sure how best to support their pupils or how to work with parents and certain issues relating to children's mental health frequently got brushed under the carpet, largely because of insufficient training. Fast forward 20 years and we are all talking about wellbeing! Schools are much better at identifying issues and working closely with parents to support their children and the Children's Commissioner has called for all schools to provide counselling for children. While it has been gratifying to see how much has changed - everywhere we look we are bombarded with so many different strategies and suggestions on how best to bring up our children -that I have long felt a "go to" book to help us is needed now, as much as a book on the importance of counselling was all those years ago. Imagine how happy I was when I first met Julie and discovered that she had been working with parents for many years in schools, delivering parent talks on sex education, sibling rivalry and wellbeing, helping parents to think, talk and openly discuss the emotional, psychological and physical needs of their children. As a nurse, psychotherapist and indeed a parent, Julie's wealth of experience and expertise is so evident throughout this impressive book. Written in her clear and accessible style, she helps us consider why our children's wellbeing is so important in a world where there are many conflicting pressures on our children. Julie helps us with practical tips on how we as parents can support, shape and nurture our children as they grow up. I wish I had had Julie's book close at hand when I was bringing up my own children to dip into from time to time and to reassure me that I was on the right track! I whole heartedly endorse Julie's book and am certain that you, and above all your children, will benefit from her wisdom.

Joanna Ebner
Headmistress,
Thomas's Kensington,
School Counsellor and
Mother of 3

About the Author

Julie Johnson originally trained as a nurse, before setting up her own business 25 years ago as a wellbeing consultant to schools. She then trained as a psychotherapist, and is now a leading provider of workshops and seminars for families in London and the surrounding area. In the last few years she has become involved in the field of mindfulness and now teaches this key life skill to children, adolescents, teachers and parents. Julie is also the author of a number of children's books on issues such as bullying, anger and step families. Julie is committed to informing, equipping, affirming and at times challenging parents as they attempt to do one of the most difficult and rewarding jobs of their lives.

WHAT
IS
WELLBEING?

Wellbeing is a word found almost everywhere these days—but what does it actually mean? It is not merely about being happy; in today's world, wellbeing refers to the state of being both physically and mentally healthy, and these have been found to be inextricably linked.

One important way of assessing your child's wellbeing is simply to ask them: how satisfied do they feel with their life? You can break it down, too: how do they feel about particular aspects of their life, such as family relationships, school or friendships? You can also look at their day-to-day moods and emotions: how do they manage their experiences on a moment-by-moment level?

Improving your child's wellbeing will help them cope with the difficulties and challenges they will inevitably face throughout their lives—and during the good times, your child will flourish.

For parents, this definition can seem a little overwhelming. Experts today are telling us that our children cannot truly be physically healthy without being mentally healthy too, and vice versa—placing a huge amount of pressure on parents to fulfil their child's every need. Of course we want our children to be comfortable, healthy and happy—but how are we supposed to achieve this all at once?

Even better, how can we educate our children as they grow and develop to see the importance of these needs for themselves, and be able to incorporate them into their lives independently? ■

IN THE KNOW

The World Health Organisation defines mental wellbeing as an individual's ability to develop their potential, work productively and creatively, build strong and positive relationships with others and contribute to their community.

MIGHT MY CHILD HAVE LOW LEVELS OF WELLBEING?

There is much debate as to whether today's children and young people are more anxious, stressed and depressed than previous generations. You may have heard stories about the sheer number of children these days, particularly girls, with mental health issues. But is it true?

Few would dispute that mental health problems are worryingly common in young people today: those most often seen include anxiety and depression, eating disorders, conduct disorder (antisocial behaviour) and self-harm. Half of all lifetime psychiatric disorders begin by the age of 14—so there's certainly no value in thinking your child is too young to be suffering from mental health problems.

These mental health conditions can affect all aspects of children's everyday lives: their ability to engage with and enjoy their education; the making of and sustaining friendships; the development of social skills.

Children who are not experiencing clinical mental health problems may still be suffering from unhealthy levels of anxiety and stress due to the fast pace of the world in which they live.

But while there are a concerning number of children experiencing mental health disorders, it is important to remember that there are also a lot of children who are happy and flourishing.

Don't worry

But you don't need to worry: the advice given in this book will help you equip your child with the skills needed to boost their own wellbeing. Most mental health problems can be helped, or even entirely prevented, simply by improving your child's levels of wellbeing. By teaching your child how to recognise triggers, how to respond and when to seek help, your child will emerge into adulthood with a strong support system—and a high level of life satisfaction. ∎

- Around 9% of children in the UK aged 8–15 report low life satisfaction.
- Girls tend to have slightly lower subjective wellbeing than boys.

Figures researched by The Children's Society

HOW CAN I IMPROVE MY CHILD'S WELLBEING?

MKOVALEVSKAYA/ISTOCK/THINKSTOCK

O ver the last few decades, there has been a movement to identify the key components of wellbeing. The science of 'positive psychology' is moving away from the old-fashioned concept of 'the pursuit of happiness' and towards a more holistic approach, based on utilising our innate physical, emotional and psychological resources (see p. 58) in order to meet our fundamental physical (see p. 15) and emotional (see p. 26) needs.

With a deeper understanding of our innate needs and resources, families, schools and communities will be better equipped to ensure the wellbeing of their children—and, indeed, all members of the community. Understanding this model also allows those who are struggling to be supported and helped in a proactive and positive way.

Give them choices

The Children's Society have been looking at the wellbeing of children in the UK over the last three years, to ▶

(see p. 58) (see p. 15) (see p. 26)

IN THE KNOW

The six priorities for promoting positive wellbeing for children:

- **The conditions to learn and develop**

- **A positive view of themselves and an identity which is respected**

- **Having enough of what matters**

- **Positive relationships with family and friends**

- **A safe and suitable home environment and local area**

- **Opportunity to take part in positive activities to thrive**

The Good Childhood Report

Family relationships are one of the most important influences on wellbeing. Children living with both parents tend to have a slightly higher level of wellbeing, but this only accounts for a 2% variation. The quality of family relationships accounts for a much more significant (20%) variation.

Figures researched by The Children's Society

pick out any important trends. When children were asked to subjectively assess their own wellbeing, a few patterns emerged, including one key aspect: the amount of choice the children believed they had in their own lives emerged as a significant factor for their sense of wellbeing.

It is enticing, the more we learn about wellbeing, to try to control our children's experiences; however, if this results in taking away your child's freedom to choose, it may have the opposite effect. ■

THIS MAY HELP

In his book **Flourish** (2011), psychologist Martin Seligman explains positive psychology and explores what makes life worth living.

Joe Griffin and Ivan Tyrell's **Human Givens: A new approach to emotional health and clear thinking** (2003) provides a thorough explanation of humans' innate needs and resources.

ZIGGY MARS/ISTOCK/THINKSTOCK

WHY IS WELLBEING IMPORTANT?

Obviously, we all want our children to be happy and healthy—but why is this particular approach so important? In order to equip your child for the world ahead, parents already have so many priorities: helping your child do well in school, for example, so that they can get a good job and lead a comfortable life.

But this approach to wellbeing is nothing new: in fact, the concepts behind it can be found in the teachings of religious and spiritual teachers from Jesus to the Buddha to Muhammad. Their teachings have since been backed up with solid psychological theory that explains why wellbeing is so important in every area of your child's life: until the basic emotional and physical needs are satisfied, higher needs such as friendship and achievement simply cannot be met.

In other words, if you want your child to do well in school, you need to focus on their mental and physical wellbeing first. ∎

THIS MAY HELP

Daniel Goleman's 1995 book **Emotional Intelligence: Why It Can Matter More Than IQ** explores how children who can manage their emotions from early in life have a better chance of success.

IS MY CHILD'S SCHOOL LOOKING AFTER THEIR WELLBEING?

One of the most important decisions we make as parents is choosing the right school for our child. Of course, you want a school that suits your child's academic ability and will help them succeed—but it also needs to support their wellbeing.

There's no single thing that you should focus on when choosing a school. What is important is that the school you pick values your child's wellbeing, and will work in partnership with you to help your child thrive.

Whether you are in the process of choosing a school or your child is currently settled in, there are a few ways you can check that the school is having a positive influence on their wellbeing.

Wellbeing programmes

Ask the school about their PSHE (personal, social, health and emotional) education, wellbeing or mindfulness programme or SRE (sex and relationship education). Pupils should be given the opportunity to consider

IN THE KNOW

"Children spend a large and formative part of their childhood at school, so it is vital schools support their mental and physical health. Good schools value pupils' wellbeing every bit as highly as academic success. Indeed, many feel that there cannot be one without the other."

MARY BREEN, HEADMISTRESS OF ST MARY'S SCHOOL ASCOT

contemporary issues around wellbeing, as well as wider issues relating to, for example, immigration, sex and relationships, and LGBTQIA+ rights. Ask how much time is given over to these topics, and what staff training is provided. You should also ask how much parents are informed about the above provisions, so that they can be prepared to discuss the issues at home while they are being explored in school. Some schools offer parent seminars which can be particularly helpful.

You might also like to ask about the school's religious education, and whether it is approached with respect for the different faiths who may be represented within the school.

Physical needs

The school should also provide a good

physical education for your child: around two hours of physical activity per week. If your child will be eating school meals, ask about the healthy eating standards. It is also worth talking to your child's teachers about how much homework they think is reasonable, and if they are concerned with their pupils getting enough rest and sleep.

Logistics

When choosing a school, you will also need to consider how logistics such as travel time will impact your child's life. It is great if your child can walk to school, at least occasionally if not every day. Time spent in the car to and from school will eat into homework time, which may make evenings too rushed; on the other hand, you could treat the time in the car as bonding time. Ideally, the school will be close enough to home that your child can develop friendships outside school hours. Do you live close enough for your child to have a friend over for a play date after school? If not, would it be feasible for them to invite a friend over for a sleepover? ■

AUTHOR'S TIPS

10 **QUESTIONS** TO ASK

1 How much prominence does the school give to **pastoral care and wellbeing**, both of pupils and staff? What training are the staff given in relation to wellbeing?

2 What is the school's **definition of wellbeing**? (The answer here should be based on attitudes, values and individuals, not on systems or statistics.)

3 Does the school have a designated **member of staff** responsible for wellbeing? Is there a counsellor, and are they available to staff and parents as well as pupils?

4 Are pupils encouraged to take part in all aspects of the school **community** (see p. 34)?

5 Which is more valued: academic success or the **experience of learning**?

6 What support is given to children who need **extra academic or emotional help**?

7 How does the school react to **differences in children**, particularly in those who do not fit the typical mould?

8 Do pupils have an opportunity to express their ideas and make suggestions or contributions that will be **valued** (see p. 38)?

9 How do parents raise **concerns**?

10 How does the school deal with **bullying**? (If the answer here is that bullying does not take place, be immediately wary. Every school will have some bullying—including cyber bullying—and you want to know that the school takes this seriously and has a system in place to support and educate all involved.)

The Parent Brief's book on UK Education provides a comprehensive guide to choosing the right school for your child.

Parents

You will have heard of the 'oxygen mask' principle: in a survival situation it is crucial that a parent secures their own oxygen mask before assisting their child. It may go against your every instinct, but you will actually then be more able to look after your child. The same principle applies here: to be able to take care of your child's needs, you need first to take care of your own.

M-IMAGEPHOTOGRAPHY/ISTOCK/THINKSTOCK

YOUR CHILD WILL LEARN FROM YOU

Children are keen observers of their parents: they will learn not only from what you teach them, but from how you behave. It is not enough simply to tell your child about following a healthy diet, getting exercise, or cultivating positive emotions: they will learn far more by watching you do these things.

WARNING SIGNS

If you are experiencing any of the following, it may be a sign that your needs are not being met. The material in the following chapters will help you make small changes that can make a huge difference. If you are experiencing five or more of these symptoms for more than two weeks, external help from a GP or therapist would be the best way forward.

- Sleep disturbance or insomnia
- Reduced appetite
- Loss of interest in things you used to enjoy
- Black and white thinking: believing everything to be your fault or responsibility; allowing worries to invade all areas of your life ('Everything is wrong!')
- Over-thinking

- Dependence on alcohol and/or illegal drugs
- A sense of disconnection from your partner, friends or family
- Anxiety or stress over things that would not normally worry you
- A sense of being out of control
- Difficulty making decisions
- Recurring panic attacks

BE COMPASSIONATE... TO YOURSELF

To be compassionate to your child, you first need a foundation of self-care. Being a parent is one of the hardest jobs on Earth, and you are bound to make a few mistakes. Take a breath and notice when you are being harshly self-critical. You can't make your child happy all the time: be gentle with yourself when you don't succeed.

LOOK AFTER YOUR OWN NEEDS

If you consistently put your child's needs above your own, they will pick up this behaviour themselves. While you would like your child to be thoughtful and considerate, it is crucial that they learn—from watching you—the importance of taking care of their own mental health.

STOCKBYTE/DIGITALVISION/THINKSTOCK

WHAT ARE OUR BASIC
HUMAN NEEDS?

Body and mind are inextricably linked; they cannot be separated from each other. In order to take care of our mind and our emotions, we need also to take care of our physical bodies. When we take care of and improve our physical wellbeing, we automatically improve our mental and emotional wellbeing. A prime example is when we exercise: not only do we strengthen our heart and lungs, but we also release endorphins—vital hormones which energise us and lift our mood.

As humans, we have an amazing number of innate resources that help us thrive (see p. 58). Our imaginations, our logic skills, even our dreams are all contributing to a healthier emotional state, with no effort needed from us. However, these mental resources only work at their best when we are looking after our physical needs.

Physical needs

The core physical needs are diet, activity and sleep. Children who are active, eat healthily and sleep well are more likely to be happy, perform better in school, feel better about themselves and their bodies, cope better with stress, and suffer less from low self-esteem, anxiety and depression. Enabling our children to establish positive attitudes towards food, activity and sleep and to develop habits early in life where they engage with all these three elements can lead to long-term healthy benefits.

Don't force it

As a parent, it can be frustrating when your child isn't committed to looking after themselves, and resists your advice. Learning to look after oneself is a journey which, as parents, we are on together with our children—acting as a guide and teacher. As important as good physical habits are, try to avoid merely forcing your child to exercise, eat and sleep well, as this will stop them from cultivating these habits in themselves. Instead, work on building your child's genuine appreciation for healthy food, a good night's sleep, and outdoor activity. ■

JACK HOLLINSWORTH/PHOTODISC/THINKSTOCK

MONKEYBUSINESSIMAGES/ISTOCK/THINKSTOCK

WHAT MAKES UP A
HEALTHY DIET?

We know how important food is for the physical wellbeing of children—but increasingly, research is telling us how important diet is for brain development, mood and general behaviour. We've all noticed that someone who is hungry may be irritable; someone with a consistently poor diet may feel generally lethargic, have low mood and find difficulty in focusing.

For many years, there has been evidence of how additives in children's diets may have an adverse effect on their behaviour; the same effects can arise from a highly processed diet. You have also no doubt heard about the importance of eating breakfast: young people who skip breakfast are starving their brain of vital nutrition and energy right at the beginning of the school day when their brains need to function well.

What you need to eat
Children need a healthy balanced diet, which includes all the key food groups (**see diagram**). Be careful how much you expose them (and even yourself) to food fads and new dietary fashions: there is a tendency for these to come and go.

Enjoying food
Children today are increasingly ▶

5 WAYS YOUR CHILD CAN ENJOY HEALTHY EATING

AUTHOR'S TIPS

1 Bring your child food shopping with you, and ask for their help in deciding on a menu. Challenge your child to put together a balanced meal of food they enjoy.

2 Cook together with your child.

3 Grow vegetables, and let your child help at every stage, from choosing what is to be grown, to planting, watering, weeding and harvesting. Families living in the city can apply for an allotment, or grow fruits, vegetables or herbs in small pots on window ledges.

4 Encourage your child to try lots of different flavours.

5 If you go out for a meal, taste each other's choices and talk about the flavours, colours and textures. You can even ask the waiter where the food comes from and how it was prepared.

Eatwell Guide

Use the Eatwell Guide to help you get a balance of healthier and more sustainable food. It shows how much of what you eat overall should come from each food group.

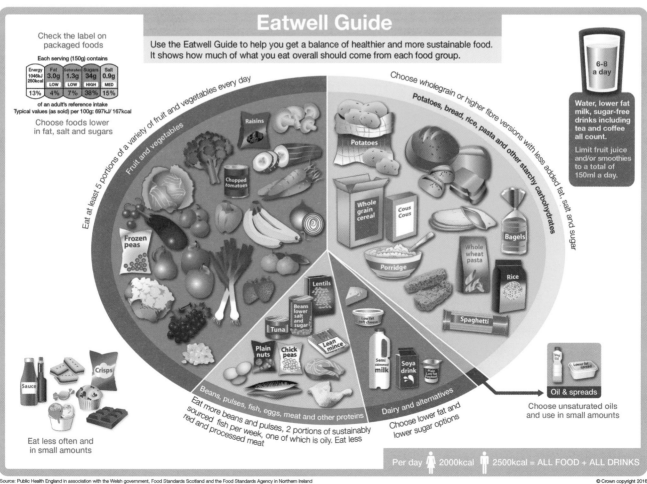

Check the label on packaged foods

Each serving (150g) contains

Energy 1046kJ 250kcal	Fat 3.0g	Saturates 1.3g	Sugars 34g	Salt 0.9g
	LOW	LOW	HIGH	MED
13%	4%	7%	38%	15%

of an adult's reference intake
Typical values (as sold) per 100g: 697kJ/ 167kcal

Choose foods lower in fat, salt and sugars

6-8 a day

Water, lower fat milk, sugar-free drinks including tea and coffee all count.

Limit fruit juice and/or smoothies to a total of 150ml a day.

Eat at least 5 portions of a variety of fruit and vegetables every day

Fruit and vegetables

Raisins

Chopped tomatoes

Frozen peas

Choose wholegrain or higher fibre versions with less added fat, salt and sugar

Potatoes, bread, rice, pasta and other starchy carbohydrates

Potatoes

Whole grain cereal

Cous Cous

Porridge

Whole wheat pasta

Bagels

Rice

Spaghetti

Lentils

Beans lower salt and sugar

Tuna

Lean mince

Plain nuts

Chick peas

Eat more beans and pulses, 2 portions of sustainably sourced fish per week, one of which is oily. Eat less red and processed meat

Beans, pulses, fish, eggs, meat and other proteins

Semi skimmed milk

Soya drink

Plain Low fat Yoghurt

Low fat soft cheese

Dairy and alternatives

Choose lower fat and lower sugar options

Oil & spreads

Choose unsaturated oils and use in small amounts

Sauce

Crisps

Eat less often and in small amounts

Per day 2000kcal 2500kcal = ALL FOOD + ALL DRINKS

THINKSTOCK

3 WAYS TO FIND TIME FOR FAMILY MEALS

1 Set the table for breakfast **the night before**. As they get older, your child can help with this. Having breakfast together at the table before heading off to school or work is a great way to start the day.

2 When your child is old enough to wait until **later in the evening** to eat, it's a good time to start routinely sharing your evening meal.

3 Make it a tradition to share a meal **over the weekend**. Sunday is often a good time for the family to come together at home—whether it's for brunch, lunch or supper.

disconnected from the food chain. Even if they do eat well, they are often unaware of the providence of their food, and are uninvolved in its preparation. Food should not merely be something to eat when it is put in front of them; it should be something to value, to appreciate and to enjoy.

Avoid setting a rule that your child has to clear their plate; it can often set up barriers to food. Instead, encourage your child to try everything on their plate, which will ensure a reasonable amount of food is eaten. Don't take it personally when your child rejects the food you have prepared: your resentment will only increase any tension surrounding mealtimes. It is also giving inappropriate attention to your child's refusal to eat, which, if your child is feeling a particular need for attention (see p. 43), may exacerbate their refusal.

Explain to your child that our taste buds change as we grow and develop, and so they may grow to love a food that they once disliked. Don't fight too hard though; if mealtimes turn into battlegrounds, this may result in your child growing up with a negative relationship to food and mealtimes.

Eat together

Sitting down to a meal together is a great way to cultivate a shared enjoyment of food, and it can also help families bond. Evidence suggests that even if a teenager doesn't speak a syllable all meal, the act of sharing a meal as a family will still help the child's confidence and ability to resist negative peer pressure. However, in our time-poor world, family meals can be an easy routine to drop. A few small changes can help you find time for a family meal even in the busiest schedule. ■

CASE STUDY: I worked with a nine-year-old boy who shared that he wished his family went less to restaurants and instead had more family nights in cooking together and playing board games. While they can be a great treat, sometimes meals at nice restaurants can place pressure on young children in relation to behaviour, and detract from their enjoyment of the food.

HOW MUCH ACTIVITY DOES MY CHILD NEED?

Children and teens aged 5–17 should accumulate at least 60 minutes of moderate-to-vigorous physical activity daily. Most of this activity should be aerobic. Vigorous activities that strengthen muscle and bone (such as running, turning or jumping) should be incorporated at least three times per week.
NHS UK RECOMMENDATIONS 2015

Activity is more than just exercise. It is important for children to take part in physical activity such as games lessons at school, recreational football, or trips to the swimming pool, but it is even more important to cultivate in children a love of being active, and taking part in activity outside.

Research from the World Health Organisation has shown that physical activity can help young people perform better academically and improve their control over symptoms of anxiety, low mood and stress, as well as assisting in their social development by providing opportunities for self-expression, interaction and integration. In general, physically active young people are more likely to adopt other healthy behaviours, such as a good diet and the avoidance of tobacco, alcohol and drug use.

For many children, lack of activity is not much of an issue when they are ▶

Even before they can stand, you can keep your baby moving throughout the day: reaching, pulling, pushing, etc.
Toddlers need at least three hours of daily activity (including standing, walking, rolling, hopping, etc.).

DESIGN PICS/THINKSTOCK

young; you may even wish they were slightly less active at times! But as they move into their teenage years, and with the ever-increasing temptation of electronics, many children are becoming increasingly sedentary at a younger and younger age.

Conflicts with your child can arise when they are not told in advance about the walk or exercise, and are interrupted from another activity they are enjoying. Plan ahead, and involve your child in the choice of what to do.

What's needed?

Activity may be made up of a variety of components: play, games, sporting activity, jobs in the home and general recreation. This activity should take

place in a few different contexts: family, school and community activities.

AUTHOR'S
TIPS

10 WAYS TO KEEP YOUR CHILD ACTIVE

1 Encourage your child to **join team sports** at school.

2 Go for **family walks**. You could prepare a quiz of what you might spot on the walk, play Hide and Seek or simply observe the trees, birds, wildlife and interesting buildings as you go.

3 Take your child **swimming** after school.

4 Hold a family **football tournament** at the weekend.

5 **Walk to school** instead of driving.

6 **Go for a picnic**, bringing a frisbee or ball to throw and catch.

7 Get your child involved in the **gardening**.

8 **Buy a trampoline.** These come in all shapes and sizes and to suit all budgets; you can even find small indoor trampolines if you don't have outside space.

9 String a net between two trees and use it for **badminton**.

10 **Rough and tumble**, not just with boys, is a good way for children to learn the boundaries of physical play.

THINKSTOCK

The importance of nature

We need nature in our lives. Many of us have lost sight of how important this is, especially those living in cities and large towns. By taking part in activity outside, and connecting with nature, we can enhance the benefits of the physical exercise we do. There is an increasing body of evidence outlining the positive influence which nature has in reducing stress levels, increasing concentration and creativity, helping to treat diseases and disorders, and promoting social cohesion. Even viewing nature from a window can improve one's mood. ■

HOW CAN MY CHILD GET ENOUGH SLEEP?

Sleep plays a vital role in good physical, mental and emotional wellbeing throughout our lives. Childhood is an important time to lay the foundations of good sleep patterns and to help our children appreciate and value this important daily experience.

During the hours that our children sleep, the body is working to support healthy brain function and maintain physical health. The way children sleep will have an effect on how they feel when they wake up: in children and teens, sleep is enabling growth and healthy brain development. Sleep, or lack of it, has been shown to affect how well children concentrate and think; in turn, this affects how they learn, react and interact with others. It is incredible that something as simple, basic and important as sleep can be taken for granted, and in some sense despised, in the 21st century. You will often hear people boasting as to how little sleep they can get away with, as if it is a skill or positive achievement. (Adults are particularly guilty of this: be careful that your child doesn't copy you here!)

How much sleep do we need?

Newborn to 2 months old	12–18 hours
3 months to 1 year old	14–15 hours
1 to 3 years old	12–14 hours
3 to 5 years old	11–13 hours
5 to 12 years old	10–12 hours
12 to 18 years old	8.5–10 hours
Adults (18+)	7.5–9 hours

> The ideal room temperature for a good night's sleep is 18°C.

During sleep

While your child sleeps, their body is able to heal and repair the heart and blood vessels and immune system. Continuous sleep problems can result in a less efficient immune system, and make your child more susceptible to illness.

During sleep, the body maintains a healthy balance of the hormones which affect sensations of hunger. Lack of sleep can result in misplaced sensations of hunger, and make it harder for your child to maintain a healthy weight. The body also monitors its reaction to insulin, the hormone which controls blood glucose (sugar) levels. Sleep deprivation is often linked to diabetes.

Particularly vital to children is the body's ability to develop and grow; the hormones involved in this growth are triggered by deep sleep. As your child grows older, these same hormones promote the repair of cells and body tissue in teenagers and adults. Therefore a good night's sleep becomes important to puberty and, once your child reaches adulthood, fertility.

After several nights of losing sleep, even a loss of just 1–2 hours per night, one's ability to function suffers as if you haven't slept at all for a day or two.

Types of sleep

There are two types of sleep: slow wave sleep (SWS) and rapid eye movement (REM). SWS is the phase of sleep during which our bodies recuperate; REM is important for learning and memory. It is during REM that we dream, and process the events of the day; throughout the night, we have about four to five periods of REM sleep.

Newborn babies spend up to 80% of ▶

10 TIPS TO HELP YOUR CHILD GET MORE SLEEP

AUTHOR'S TIPS

1 An evening rhythm and **routine** can help your child get ready to sleep.

2 **Warm milk or lavender are both natural relaxants.**

3 **Mindfulness** and calming techniques **(see p. 90).**

4 Your child needs time to **relax** and de-stress after school, and after finishing their homework.

5 **Looking at screens around bedtime can make it harder to get a good night's sleep. Your child should turn off electronics an hour before going to sleep.**

6 The bedroom should just be for sleeping; avoid putting a computer or TV there. If you don't have enough space in your home for a study area outside the bedroom, set up a clear **separate space for work**, and discourage your child from ever working on their bed.

7 Keep the bedroom **quiet**. If your child is disturbed by noise from a nearby road, for example, they might like to try using earplugs.

8 **Ensure their room is a good temperature: too hot, and your child may suffer restless sleep; too cold, and they may have nightmares, or struggle to sleep at all.**

9 Thick curtains, blinds or eye masks can aid with the **darkness** your child needs to sleep.

10 A soft **night light** can be helpful for a child who is scared of the dark.

SHOULD WE HAVE A **NO PHONES** RULE?

There is a huge amount of evidence that technology in the bedroom is not healthy for children or adults. Excessive screen time can disrupt your child's sleep patterns, and children who use laptops in their bedrooms may end up isolating themselves from their family. Do be sensitive to the fact that technology is an important part of your child's social life, as it can be upsetting when parents don't acknowledge this. However, you should set clear rules and boundaries surrounding the use of technology—both your child's and your own! A 'no phones in the bedroom' rule is a particularly good idea, or even 'no screen time up to an hour before bedtime'.

---

their sleep in the REM phase, due to the need for rapid learning and skill development. As children grow and develop, this gradually decreases to about 20–25% in adult life. Stress and anxiety will increase REM sleep as the brain is attempting to process its worries; a stressed child may report having more dreams and nightmares. Of course, if a child is having more REM sleep, they are having less of the restorative slow wave sleep, and their immune system will be weakened. Therefore, getting 'enough' sleep may not be as simple as getting the prescribed number of hours (which vary from person to person anyway, depending on personal circadian rhythms): the quality of sleep will make a huge difference to your child's wellbeing. Talking through and soothing your child's worries before bedtime will help them get a better night's sleep.

Light and sleep hygiene

From TVs with increasingly large screens to computers, tablets and e-readers, the amount of artificial light in our homes is rising. Even with the interior lights off, those living in the city may find street light streaming in.

This amount of artificial light can get in the way of our bodies' natural release of melatonin: a hormone secreted as daylight fades in order to prepare us for sleep. Melatonin release is particularly inhibited by exposure to blue lights, such as those emitted by smartphone, laptop, e-reader or tablet screens. If your child is not releasing melatonin, they will have difficulty sleeping.

To counter this, you can reduce your child's access to screens in the evenings (watching TV or films is especially negative as the fast editing can keep your child's mind working overtime all night), or download an app such as f.lux to reduce the blue light. Consider installing black-out blinds or curtains in your child's bedroom, and avoid very bright or LED lights in your child's bathroom: this is where they will spend a considerable amount of time just before bed. If these lights can't be avoided entirely, try turning down the intensity, or balancing out any harsh blue lights with warmer lights in the same room. ∎

> In a study of 10,000 16 to 19-year-olds, researchers in Norway found that the longer a young person spent looking at an electronic screen before going to bed, the worse quality sleep they were likely to have.

THIS MAY HELP

You can download various apps and computer programs, such as f.lux, to reduce the blue light emitted by screens, allowing you to use technology at night with less effect on your sleep.

Parents

For many parents, life is already so busy that things like fitting in regular physical activity, preparing healthy meals, and getting a good night's sleep can become a low priority—or even be seen as a luxury. But the consequences of ignoring these needs are not trivial, and can elevate your risk of illnesses from diabetes to depression.

THINKSTOCK

TAKE TIME TO ENJOY FOOD

Working parents will be aware of the temptation to eat lunch at their desks—it can even be a badge of honour!—but as a habit, this is unhealthy for both your body and mind. The same applies for parents at home during the day: if you take time to value, enjoy and appreciate your meals, you will pass on this same healthy approach to your children. Besides, parenting is a highly demanding role—and so you need the brainpower!

ASK YOURSELF...

Am I setting a good example? Does my child observe me constantly dieting or obsessing over my looks or weight?

SLEEP TIPS FOR PARENTS WITH BABIES

New parents may feel the need to get chores done whenever their baby is sleeping in the day. Instead, catch up on much-needed sleep of your own. You can let the household jobs slide. Don't set unrealistic standards or expectations for yourself.

- Take daytime naps when possible.
- Accept that life will be different for a few months.
- If you have other children, try as much as possible to work out a new rhythm to the day, as the one you had before may not work.
- Allow yourself and your baby to find your own way, not based on anyone else's experiences.

GET MOVING

- Walk as much as possible. For those living in cities, walking can actually save you time.
- Get off public transport one stop early and walk.
- Use the stairs instead of the lift, and walk up escalators.
- Schedule in a short walk, or regular daily activity such as swimming, running or yoga. Even better, make these a family activity.

MAKE THE BEDROOM JUST RIGHT

Bedrooms are for sleep and sex (if we're lucky)! Watching TV, checking emails, or using your phone in the bedroom gives mixed messages to your brain about what the bedroom is for. It also helps if your mattress and pillows are as comfortable as possible. Some beds accommodate two different types of mattress for couples with different tastes.

WHAT ARE THE FUNDAMENTAL EMOTIONAL NEEDS?

ANDREAS RODRIGUEZ/ISTOCK/THINKSTOCK

All children (and all humans) have fundamental emotional needs; when these are not being met, even children who are well-fed, physically healthy, wealthy and well-educated may report a low level of wellbeing. Even parents who care very deeply about their children may inadvertently be depriving them of their emotional needs: by trying to protect them from any discomfort, embarrassment or unhappiness, they are actually denying them the experience to grow emotionally.

Our emotional needs are all interconnected, but they can be divided into nine key areas: security, control, community, respect, intimacy, attention, privacy, achievement and meaning in life—each of which are covered in this chapter. Cultivating positive emotions (see p. 58) is also crucial for your child's emotional wellbeing.

Take it easy

In many ways, caring for your child's emotional needs is more challenging than supporting their physical needs: it requires you to manage your own feelings of anger, frustration and even tiredness.

You won't get it right all the time: no parent ever can. This chapter will give you a useful overview of your child's needs and how you can meet them—but don't berate yourself any time you overreact or poorly manage a situation. Remember: you are a human with emotional needs of your own. ■

HOW CAN I HELP MY CHILD FEEL **CONFIDENT AND SAFE?**

All humans share an innate emotional need for security: both physical and psychological. This might refer to security in our relationships, in our school or workplace, in our community; it might refer to knowing we have a roof over our heads. When someone's inherent sense of security is under threat, they will feel anxious or stressed, or overcompensate by developing an unhealthy dependence on the things which do make them feel secure.

While we all share this basic need,

the level of security we need can vary significantly between individuals. For some children, changes such as moving house or school can make them feel insecure (see p. 73); other children may find this level of change stimulating. Working out your child's security needs, and ensuring they are met, is crucial in raising them to feel confident and safe, even through life's most difficult challenges.

Emotional connections

While we all know how important it is to give our children physical security

(keeping a roof over their heads, keeping them safe from physical harm), far more complex and varied is their need for emotional security.

In fact, emotional security is so innate a need for children (and humans in general) that you will notice babies seeking out emotional connections from the moment they are born, by imitating the facial expressions they see. If, for example, a parent sticks out their tongue at their baby, the baby will often stick out its own tongue in exchange; not only is this adorable, it also reflects an innate need for this ▶

6 THINGS CHILDREN NEED TO FEEL SECURE

1 The feeling they are **loved** for who they are.

2 The experience of being **listened to**—and having their thoughts and feelings respected (even if they seem childish or difficult).

3 The knowledge that they will be **supported** (but not necessarily rescued) through difficult life experiences, big or small.

4 The freedom to **express themselves** without being dismissed or ridiculed.

5 **Boundaries** and consequences that help them learn from their mistakes.

6 Encouragement to **take risks**.

baby to form connections.

When you pause to consider how deep the need for connection, affection and protection really runs, it's unsurprising that an overall sense of security is hugely important for your child.

Developing independence

Parents will no doubt be keen that their child can be independent—and may worry that keeping them overly secure and protected will hinder this. In actual fact, a child who feels safe within a secure family setting is usually more able to express their autonomy and move out from that safe foundation—and there's an important reason for this.

Fulfilling a child's need for emotional security will allow them to see themselves as loved and valued for who they are (not just what they achieve). A child who innately feels secure will be more confident expressing themselves and trying new things—as they are not afraid of losing others' support.

Of course, as humans we do need to be taken out of our comfort zones; it is important that children are encouraged to stretch themselves. The vital thing is that throughout any new challenges, children retain one crucial sense of security: that of feeling cared for.

Routine and structure

One way to help young children feel secure is by giving them routines, so that they can anticipate what is happening from day to day and week to week. Try to keep their morning routine the same: when they wake up, when they have breakfast, when they leave the house for school, etc. After school, keep to a routine as far as possible, allowing for variations such as after-school activities. Part of their evening schedule might involve preparing their things for the next day—giving an overall sense of structure to their week.

There are multiple benefits to this. Firstly, when children know what is expected of them, this can lessen the need for nagging and arguments. Secondly, and perhaps counter-intuitively, having a strong routine can actually make children more comfortable with change. This is because the security that routines give to young children helps them develop confidence in their surroundings, which in turn enables them to cope better with new experiences.

Note, though, that it is crucial your family routines are communicated explicitly to your child. When children are expected to follow a schedule that they don't understand, and have no control over, it can result in outright conflict within the family. As your child gets older, you can work together with them to set a routine that everybody is happy with.

Family rules

As a parent, you will have your own ideas about what behaviour is or isn't acceptable—and much of your parenting will naturally be based on this. Easygoing, compliant children may work out fairly quickly what the rules are; stronger-willed children may struggle to fall in line. But both personality types (and everything in between) will thrive when family rules are made explicit before children are expected to obey them.

It is important that everyone in charge of childcare is involved in setting the rules, that these rules are communicated to all involved (including the nanny, au pair, or grandparents) and that caregivers do not undermine each other. Otherwise, children who have been told 'no' by one parent (or caregiver) may appeal to the other for a different answer. Children may find a thrill in 'getting away with things' with a less strict caregiver, but this inconsistency is

> "I love change. It's really exciting never knowing what will happen next. That's how I feel about growing up."
>
> SOPHIE, 10

> "I like things to stay just as they are, so I know where I am. I'm sad about growing up, I won't be a kid anymore. I like being a kid."
>
> BEN, 11

GMAST3R/ISTOCK/THINKSTOCK

actually damaging their innate sense of security—especially if they then witness arguments between their parents or carers.

There's no right answer for how to discipline children when they break the rules—but it is crucial that you remain consistent, and that your child understands why they are being punished. A great starting point after bad behaviour is to ask your child what they think they have done wrong. If an appropriate consequence has been agreed upon, follow through. If you overreact and set an inappropriate punishment, calmly explain to your child that you were upset, and on reflection have decided on a different consequence. You may even talk to your child about what they think the consequence should be.

It's worth noting that a child acting up may be a sign that their need for security is not being met. What seems like defiance and rebellion may in fact be an uncertain child trying to figure out their boundaries. Bad behaviour may also be a form of attention seeking: if a child is feeling a lack of emotional security, then they will even crave disapproval over being ignored. If you think this is the case, consider how you can rebalance family life, and give your child more attention and reassurance.

Don't compare children to each other in terms of their behaviour. Remember particularly that girls can be up to three years ahead of boys in emotional development. ∎

AUTHOR'S TIPS

5 CREATIVE WAYS
TO SET RULES

1 **Brainstorm** the rules that your own family had, and which ones you found helpful or unhelpful. Share this process with your partner or co-parent.

2 Make **positive statements** rather than 'dos and don'ts': let your children know what is expected of them, rather than a list of restrictions.

3 **Communicate** your family's rules clearly to all involved, perhaps displayed as a poster.

4 **Review** the rules: as children mature, they can become more involved in family discussion about how the rules may or may not be working. You might even let them suggest some rules of their own.

5 Set a good example: **parents** need to keep to the rules as well. If you say no screens at the table, that means you too!

HOW MUCH CONTROL SHOULD I LET MY CHILD HAVE?

TOMWANG122/ISTOCK/THINKSTOCK

One innate emotional need all humans share is the need for control and autonomy. In other words, humans need to feel they are able to make their own choices about their own lives.

For children, particularly very young ones, this is a difficult thing to manage. While children are not yet old enough to make informed decisions, parents will need to make choices on their behalf—

and yet by controlling their every moment, parents risk stifling their need for autonomy.

All parents have experienced or

As children get older they may start to overcompensate for a lack of control in one area of their lives

heard of the 'terrible twos', the period when a child is around two years old and begins to challenge a parent's authority. It may be difficult, but it's

also an incredibly important and exciting stage in a child's development: this is the moment children start expressing their desire to make choices! Imagine being told at every moment of every day what to do and how to do it. This total lack of control would, of course, lead to serious anxiety and stress. No wonder two-year-olds can be so difficult! Rather than becoming even firmer when a child throws a tantrum,

eating, or in extreme cases, for eating disorders: young people struggling with a lack of autonomy may exercise an obsessive form of control over what they eat.

Finding a balance

As with all of the core human needs, it is important to find a balance. While a lack of control can lead, in extreme cases, to anxiety and depression, individuals who seek too much control may find themselves stressed when not everything goes their way—and this can be stressful for those around them too!

Giving a child too much choice may leave them feeling insecure (see p. 27); exerting too much control over their lives restricts their experience, and prevents them from learning how to take responsibility. Somewhere in between the two is the perfect balance: giving your child a stable base from which they can explore the world themselves.

Give your reasons

As a parent, there will obviously be times you need to put your foot down and tell your child what to do. On these occasions, always explain clearly what it is you would like your child to do and why. If your child has a good understanding of why they are being required to act in a certain way, this will help them regain a sense of control over their actions.

When you and your child talk openly, you may even find you are comfortable giving them a higher level of choice than you had thought.

When conflict arises, demonstrate a recognition and understanding of your child's perspective. This doesn't mean you're agreeing with (or even condoning) their feelings, but your child will benefit from feeling your empathy, ▶

remember that they are most likely trying to express an inner frustration that they don't have the language skills to communicate. Don't reward their aggressive behaviour, but consider that you might have been exerting too much control over them in order to prompt that response.

As children get older, they may start to overcompensate for a lack of control in one area of their lives (perhaps home or school) by strictly controlling another—particularly if they are perfectionists. You will probably have heard that this can be a trigger for fussy

9 DECISIONS TO LET **YOUR** CHILD MAKE
AUTHOR'S TIPS

1 What **food** to eat. You might insist your child eats five fruit and vegetables a day, for example, but let them choose which ones.

2 What **clothes** to wear, within reason.

3 What **games** to play.

4 Who to be **friends** with. (Avoid manipulating their choices.)

5 Which relatives to greet with **a hug**.

6 Which **TV programmes, books and music** to enjoy (as long as you feel they are age appropriate).

7 What their **interests** are. There may be a certain level of schoolwork you expect them to do, but allow them to dictate which interests they wish to follow further.

8 How much **privacy** they have—particularly as they get older.

9 What **opinions** they hold—though parents should respectfully challenge these opinions, particularly racist, homophobic or insensitive attitudes.

A UCL research study tracked the wellbeing of more than 5,000 participants born in 1946. People whose parents repeatedly invaded their privacy and/or carried out simple tasks for them were more likely to score low in the wellbeing surveys, when assessed in their teens, their 30s and 40s, and even their 60s.

"I believe children should have some say over their lives, even when they are toddlers, so I always wanted my children to feel they had choices. It might be that, if we were going on a trip, I would ask them where they wanted to go—but of course I'd make sure both options worked for me. Or it might just be that I offered them two options for vegetables for their evening meal! Even when I was imposing rules, I tried to give them an element of choice: for example, when they were becoming fussy eaters, I told them that they were allowed up to six foods each that they wouldn't eat, but no more. It worked brilliantly: my previously picky daughters suddenly ate happily—because they felt they had some control."

CLAIRE, MOTHER OF TWO GROWN-UP DAUGHTERS

even if you then overrule them.

A classic example is when, during an argument, one child declares they 'hate' their sibling or parent. It can be very upsetting to hear these aggressive statements, and it is tempting to demand an apology at once, whether your child wants to issue it or not. Instead, pause to acknowledge the very real emotions at play here. With sensitivity to your child's feelings, explain why you are asking them to apologise. Once your child feels listened to and understood, they will be more able to issue a genuine apology—rather than feeling silenced and controlled.

Encourage self-sufficiency

Your child will feel a greater sense of control over their life the more tasks they feel able to complete by themselves. Resist immediately helping with every challenge your child faces: even if it's as minor as them asking you to open a jar for them, or to tie their shoelaces. Respond instead with encouragement; even if they fail or make mistakes, the attempt alone will increase their confidence. If you lovingly talk through what went wrong, and praise the effort they put in, they may even start actively looking forward to the next time they can have another go.

Try actively seeking out little challenges for them—such as 'Can you pour out this juice for me?' Even if they spill it, praise their efforts. As your child gets older, the challenges might be laying the table, feeding the dog, loading and unloading the dishwasher, or making dinner for the family—or you might encourage them to explore a craft project of their own. Don't put down any ideas that you consider to be silly or immature; be curious about your child's individual vision and explore with them where they might take it.

A word about obedience and resistance

Some children are naturally easy-going and obedient; as a parent, these children can seem on the surface much easier to handle. You may find yourself praising your child for 'always doing what you ask', or criticising a strong-willed child for 'always having to argue'.

JUPITERIMAGES/BANANASTOCK/THINKSTOCK

Be wary about this comparison. You may find your strong-willed child difficult, but you would be delighted if they stood up to a negative peer group. On the other hand, if your compliant child has always been rewarded for doing as they are asked, they might be more easily pressurised and led astray by their friends.

Instead of valuing one personality type over the other, actively encourage autonomy in both personality types. The naturally obedient child will then be better able to make their own decisions about whose orders to follow, and the strong-willed child will be less likely to resist your requests if they feel you respect and value them. ■

AUTHOR'S TIPS

WHAT'S WRONG WITH 'HELICOPTER PARENTING'

'Helicopter parenting' means paying extremely close attention to your child's experiences and remaining closely involved at all times, even when your child is at school. As a parent who cares enormously about your child's future, you're only trying to help. The problem is that 'helicopter parenting' doesn't allow your child to have any autonomy over their life. You may find them fighting back against your well-intentioned support, which can be hurtful; just remember that it is natural (and wonderful!) that your child should wish to make their own decisions and mistakes. In the short term you may be solving problems for them—but in the longer term, they will struggle to regulate their experiences on their own.

By encouraging your child's autonomy, you are showing that you trust and respect them. A child who feels supported in this way is more likely to come to you for advice anyway!

HOW CAN I BUILD A STRONG COMMUNITY FOR MY CHILD?

Humans are social animals: we function best when part of a group. For thousands of years, humans lived and thrived in small close-knit communities. Children were considered the responsibility of the whole village, not just of their parents. There was an evolutionary reason for this: in the days when parents often died before their children reached adulthood, this provided children with a support system to fall back on (which increased their chance of survival).

But there's another reason too, one which remains relevant even today. Along the journey from childhood to adulthood, your child will need to learn the practical skills to survive in adult life—but also the social and emotional skills. When your child emerges as a new adult into the world, you will want them to form relationships based on cooperation and trust, something which requires a certain level of emotional intelligence. As a parent, you will play a crucial role in the development of your child's social skills—but you can't do it alone. Emotional intelligence is learned by interacting with a rich tapestry of people, and gaining exposure to different personalities, beliefs, backgrounds and life experiences.

Finally, community directly contributes to one's immediate sense of wellbeing. Not only does a community offer support during hard times, it is also beneficial in the sharing of achievements and reminiscing about shared experiences. A community can make us feel connected to the world around us, and without it, we may feel isolated and anxious.

The expression 'It takes a village to raise a child' can be found in many forms in various African languages—but in the UK, our experience as parents could hardly be more different. The industrial revolution has changed the landscape of the UK, and of other industrialised countries, beyond recognition. Many people live a long way from their families, and close communities are rare. A strong community for your child is no longer something you can take for granted; it's something you will have to build.

Where to start

Although strong inbuilt communities like those of our ancestors are rare, you will no doubt have naturally built a few small communities over the course of your life so far. You may have friends through work, through the parents at your child's school or your ante-

> In the few small tribes which still survive, evidence of depression is virtually nonexistent. When a member of these tribes is struggling, it will be quickly noticed—and help is close at hand. In Amish and Hutterite communities, each member has a responsibility to the tribe, not just to themselves. The result of this is that the giving and receiving of support and care are of equal importance.

natal group, through your local pub or church, choir or football team—or you may even have found a group of friends online, perhaps on Mumsnet.

For children, their need for community and connection will initially be met within the extended family. As they grow and develop, they will gravitate towards communities of their own. Just as your own need for community and connection will naturally have driven you to form bonds with colleagues or neighbours, your child will naturally seek out a group of school friends, or friends from a football team, choir or drama group.

Befriend the neighbours

With the loss of many local shops, and the decline of community hubs such as the village church or local pub, the concept of neighbourhood has changed dramatically over the last few decades. These days we are far more likely to hop in our car instead of walk, visit the big impersonal supermarket instead of the local market, or to shop entirely online. ▶

IN THE KNOW

"The power of community to create health is far greater than any physician, clinic or hospital."
MARK HYMAN, PHYSICIAN

5 PLACES YOUR CHILD CAN FIND
CONNECTION AND COMMUNITY

1 When choosing a **nursery school**, remember that this will likely be your child's first main community outside the family. Try to find a school where your child will meet a diverse range of children, and where the teachers seem to form genuine relationships with their students.

2 After-school **clubs or activities** are a great place to find new friends for your child.

3 A **nanny or au pair** can give your child an important sense of connection when you have to be at work.

4 Your child may form a connection with any **home help** that you employ. (Don't forget to warn your child before any of these people move on from their jobs with you, and involve the child in saying goodbye.)

5 Pay attention to what is happening in your **local community**: are there volunteering opportunities? Are there any activities on offer? Some communities even host small festivals: think about how your family can contribute.

"Every New Year our family does a 'bittersweet' review of the year. We put a large sheet of paper in the middle of the table, and write down everything that has been sad or difficult (or 'bitter'). We take it in turns to talk through what we've written down and listen to each other; sometimes there will be tears. Then we turn the paper over to the 'sweet' side, and write down all our happy memories and proud achievements. We started this when my sons were in junior school, and still do it over 15 years later, now they have families of their own. We feel very fortunate that the sweet always outweighs the bitter, even in the years that have brought bereavements— although perhaps this is because we've taken the time to notice and honour both bitter and sweet moments in our lives together."

JENNY, PARENT AND GRANDPARENT

Try making an effort to greet your neighbours whenever you pass them, and even to invite them over for a drink. Take the time to walk around the neighbourhood and notice what is actually there: a local coffee shop that you've never visited, perhaps, or a family-run corner shop. Involve your child in this: it will give them the sense that they are part of a wider community outside the walls of their own house.

They may particularly enjoy a visit to the local park or playground; even if you have a garden of your own, this is a great way to meet other children and families.

Talk to your child about how the community is supported, and by whom: the road cleaners, dustbin collectors, GP surgeries, and local shopkeepers.

Community on the Internet

Over the last 20 years or so, the

PAUL/THINKSTOCK

DIGITALVISION/THINKSTOCK

5 RITUALS YOU MIGHT INTRODUCE— OR INVENT YOUR OWN!

1 **Family night**. This could entail a special meal that the family have prepared together, or perhaps you could all choose a film to watch, or a board game to play.

2 Depending on your belief system, you might introduce some form of **spiritual ritual**, whether it's saying a prayer, lighting a candle, or reading a poem.

3 Think about how your family will celebrate major **rites of passage** such as starting school, reaching a certain age or finishing exams: it could be a photo taken in a specific location, or a celebratory meal at a favourite restaurant.

4 A **family scrapbook** or memory box, compiled through the years, can make a lovely gift for a child on their 18th birthday. Include celebrations of your child's personal projects as well as family memories.

5 **One-on-one** bonding time between a parent and child is very special: perhaps one parent could take a child for a weekend away to mark key milestones. Not only does this ritual enhance the sense of community within the family as a whole, it will also meet your child's need for intimacy (see p. 41).

emergence of the Internet has formed a new global community—but can it satisfy our emotional needs in the same way? For children growing up today, this digital world will be hugely important (see p. 84). Your child may form strong and genuine connections with young people that they never actually meet in person—and we should not devalue these connections just because we don't understand them.

However, the name 'social media' can be misleading: often, excessive use of social networking sites can actually contribute to a sense of isolation. As people tend to post only the positive parts of their life online, social media can engender a level of self-comparison: 'Why am I not as popular?', 'Why am I not as happy?' or perhaps 'Why wasn't I invited to that event?'

Social media sites are increasingly aimed at younger and younger children, and wisdom is required when deciding at what age you will allow your child to sign up.

Family rituals

Rituals and traditions provide meaning and a sense of community to family life. These are distinct from everyday routines, which provide a sense of security (see p. 27); rituals instead convey a symbolic sense of belonging. ∎

> "Being a parent is such a learning curve. Over the years, I've found it helpful to chat with others, to share and discuss problems as well as highlights with them. It might be strategies to encourage a child to do their homework, or advice if your child is being teased at school. Often, simple advice from other parents can lead to effective solutions that might not at first seem obvious to you."
>
> **MELANIE, MOTHER OF FOUR**

HOW CAN I MAKE MY CHILD FEEL VALUED?

Humans need to feel accepted, valued and appreciated for the contribution we bring to our community—be it our family, friendship group, workplace or perhaps a sports team. As a society, we tend to give status and respect to those who are well-known, who are rich or who have reached the top of their profession—and ignore those whose achievements are less obvious.

We can also put too much emphasis on demonstrating status through possessions—depending on your child's age, this may be their toys, their clothes or the family car—but these outward symbols of status are ultimately superficial. There is nothing intrinsically wrong with your child taking pride in their material possessions, but make sure that they are not setting their value by these things.

In fact, you don't want your child to set too much value on what others think of them at all. Instead, you want them to develop an inner sense of self-worth—but do acknowledge that it is a fundamental part of human nature to desire the respect of others.

Children in society

The status of children within society will also affect how much respect your child feels they are getting. Luckily, we have moved on a lot from the days when children were to be 'seen and not heard'—but traces of this attitude still remain. You may find certain places or friendship circles to be very

---

THIS MIGHT HELP

Look up the Myers Briggs Type Indicator (MBTI) test. This test sorts individuals into one of 16 personality types, and can be very useful in understanding how people from each personality type function.

THIS MIGHT HELP

Susan Cain's book **Quiet: The Power of Introverts in a World That Can't Stop Talking** is a great resource to help you understand your introverted child.

TAYLOR HINTON/ISTOCK/THINKSTOCK

GPOINTSTUDIO/ISTOCK/THINKSTOCK

4 WAYS TO SHOW YOUR CHILD YOU RESPECT THEM

1 **Avoid comparing** your child to their siblings or peers; value them for who they are as an individual.

2 Give them **jobs and responsibilities**: even very young children can be involved in tidying up, for example. For busy parents, it may seem quicker to do things yourself—but this deprives your child of the feeling that they make a valued contribution to family life. (Older children may grumble—but as long as you have only set them a reasonable number of jobs, they will still benefit!)

3 Take an interest in their **hobbies**. Your child may just introduce you to new activities that you didn't know you enjoyed!

4 **Listen** to their thoughts and feelings, and show a genuine interest even if you do not agree.

unwelcoming to children; consider the effect this will have on your child's estimation of their own value.

Of course, you are bound to want 'grown up time' away from the children. At these times, explain to your child that it is important for you to spend time alone with your friends, just as they need to spend time with their friends away from parents.

Respect your child for who they are

It is important that we respect each of their unique talents and little idiosyncrasies. One way we can do this is by reflecting on what their personality type may be. This does not ▶

AUTHOR'S TIPS

HOW TO TREAT YOUR...

INTROVERT

- Respect their need for privacy.
- Never embarrass them in public—whether it's praise or a reprimand.
- Give them time to think: don't demand an instant answer.
- Don't interrupt them. Give them warnings to finish what they are doing.
- Let them work alone.
- Introverts still need touch, but take a gentler approach. Don't get upset by a child who's not as cuddly.

EXTRAVERT

- Respect their independence.
- Compliment them in the company of others.
- Encourage their enthusiasm, and allow them to talk things through.
- Plan exciting surprises for them.
- Offer them opinions.
- Make physical and verbal gestures of affection.
- Accept their bouncy 'Tigger-like' tendencies.

CASE STUDY: I worked with a father whose ten-year-old son said that he felt that he was not the son his father wanted. The father admitted that he spent more time with his younger son, who shared the same hobbies as him, but he was very saddened to hear the older son's feelings: he felt he had tried to share his interests equally with both sons.

At a parent seminar, the father learned the importance of being willing to move into our children's worlds. Instead of trying to share his own hobbies with his oldest son, who had different interests, the father tried his son's hobbies instead. As the son then felt valued and respected by his father, their relationship transformed.

JOLIEO/ISTOCK/THINKSTOCK

mean you should put your child in a box and define them by it—but it can form a useful framework for getting to understand your child.

For example, it might help you recognise that your child is more introverted than extraverted. Once you understand this, you can stop mistaking their quietness for a lack of confidence, and instead appreciate that more introverted children need a little extra time to think before they speak. An introverted child will feel respected if you treat them with patience, and show that you value their answers enough to wait for them.

Of course, nobody's personality can be explained that simply. Your child's personality type merely shows their innate preferences—but it shouldn't constrain them. An introverted child can absolutely practise extraversion when needed, just as a bouncy extraverted child can sit still and quietly when they are asked. Both children may do this very successfully, though they might find it draining. ∎

"When our daughter was nine, we took her to visit a family therapist to find out why she was so much quieter than her younger brother. My partner and I have always been very loud and outgoing, and our son clearly takes after us. Our daughter, on the other hand, would be very reserved and shy whenever we had friends round. We'd also been contacted by her school, who were concerned about her lack of confidence as she rarely contributed in class.

The therapist helped us realise that our daughter is an introvert who prefers to listen carefully and think before she speaks. She's actually a very wise and thoughtful little girl who knows herself very well; when asked by the therapist to describe herself, she did so with no hesitancy. At parties, we now encourage her to engage one-on-one with a few people instead of expecting her to be as bubbly as her brother. At school, she needs time to think about what she's learned before being asked to contribute her thoughts.

Our society has a clear preference for extraverts like my partner and myself—but now we understand our daughter so much better, we have learned to value her wonderful introverted qualities."

JACK, FATHER OF TWO

FUNDUCK/ISTOCK/THINKSTOCK

HOW CAN I BUILD AN INTIMATE RELATIONSHIP WITH MY CHILD?

The human desire for intimacy is a powerful driving force in our lives. While having a wide community of acquaintances (**see p. 34**) can make us feel better connected to the world, we also crave the knowledge that at least one other person, whether it's a romantic partner, family member or close friend, knows us inside out—and still accepts us. We want to laugh and cry with this person, to share our thoughts and feelings, or to sit in companionable silence.

Different personality types will require different amounts of intimacy, but we all need some level of intimacy in our lives. Most people will experience a sense of stress or loneliness when their need for intimacy is not being met—but some people may find themselves drained and exhausted when they spend too much time emotionally connected with others. ▶

(see p. 34)

AUTHOR'S TIPS

DO BOYS AND GIRLS **NEED DIFFERENT LEVELS** OF INTIMACY?

There has been much debate about whether being male or female affects the amount of intimacy that each human needs. The stereotype says that girls need to talk about their feelings in a way that boys don't—but this can be very damaging. It is suggested that the disproportionately high suicide rates amongst males may be due to the expectation that men will always suppress their feelings; they are therefore less likely to seek emotional help.

All humans have a need for intimacy—and it is different personalities that tend to affect how much, rather than different genders. Whatever the gender of your child, make it clear that you are there to listen to any thoughts and feelings they would like to share.

AUTHOR'S
TIPS

3 WAYS TO DEVELOP INTIMACY

1 Take notice of the small ways your child is trying to attract your **attention**, and respond with an affirmation or a warm smile—or work out if it's something that requires more time.

2 Give your child some **one-on-one** attention. In your busy family life, this may not happen spontaneously; think about how you can deliberately create time for each child individually.

3 Listen to their **hopes and dreams**, however outlandish they may seem. Don't dismiss these dreams, no matter how childish or unrealistic they may seem.

Physical intimacy

Human touch is believed to have a wide range of physical and emotional benefits: various studies have suggested a correlation between physical touch and pain reduction, improved immune systems and even lower blood glucose.

The emotional benefits you have likely seen for yourself. Physical touch can reduce anxiety and improve our positive outlook; this is why it feels soothing to be hugged or touched.

Touch is the earliest form of intimacy between a parent and child, but as children grow into teenagers, they begin to shy away from this sort of physical intimacy—just when they need it the most!

Developing intimacy

Forming intimate relationships isn't straightforward; it requires empathy (see p. 61) from both sides. To build an intimate relationship, you must be able to read other people's moods, read your own mood and understand how it might be affecting others,

and to respond empathetically to others' experiences—even if you don't necessarily agree with how the other person has behaved.

If you keep an eye out for it, you'll notice that your child makes daily small bids for your attention (**see p. 43**). This might mean asking for a cuddle, trying to sit on your lap or wanting to play; it might mean acting up and being naughty. Either way, reacting to these with warmth is a key ingredient to building an intimate relationship; even if it is just with a smile, a nod, or a touch, you are showing your child that you acknowledge and value their feelings.

If your child feels confident that you are there to listen to them when they talk about trivial things, then they will trust you to be there for their more intimate thoughts.

It will also help your child to see you demonstrate physical and emotional intimacy (through both physical touch and close communication) with your

co-parent or with other key figures in your and their lives.

Stand back

No matter how wonderful your relationship with your child is, it should not be the sole intimate relationship in their life. As they grow older, you should fully expect and encourage them to form close relationships with a varied circle of friends and eventually partners. Do not be hurt when your child turns to their friends or other adults instead of you when they want someone to confide in, or share with; this is a very natural part of growing up. Stand back and allow these other intimate relationships to develop, but make sure your child knows you'll still be there for them when they need you. ■

HOW MUCH ATTENTION DOES MY CHILD NEED?

It's easy to feel irritated by a child seeking attention. We may get cross, prompting an even worse reaction from the child. Or we may ignore them, leaving them to withdraw with this basic need unfulfilled. The phrase 'attention-seeking' is usually used negatively—but once you understand attention as a fundamental human need, you realise that a child seeking attention is every bit as valid as a hungry child seeking food. And the reality, inconvenient though it may be for busy parents, is that children need a lot of attention.

Children who do not receive enough quality attention from a young age may play up, or may seek it instead from others—inappropriately crossing the usual boundaries set by teachers or friends, for example. In both of these examples, they tend to be 'rewarded' with the attention they were after—meaning that this behaviour will be reinforced.

Try instead to give your child attention when they are behaving well. When you are with your child, try to be fully present. If a distraction takes your attention away, explain to your child what you are doing and reassure them that you will give them attention as soon as you can.

You may like to practise mindfulness (see p. 90) to ensure that you are more present in your day-to-day life, and are able to notice the important moments. Give your child positive attention whenever you notice good behaviour, not just when they do what you explicitly asked them to do. If you see them being thoughtful, kind or considerate, or when you see that they have tried their best, this is a great time to give them praise (see p. 51).

'Doing' attention vs connected attention

It's not always easy to notice when you're not giving your child enough attention. After all, in between taking them from A to B, making their dinner, supervising their homework and getting them to bed, it feels like they take up your attention from morning to night. But what kind of attention really is this? Where is your mind when you are busy doing so much for them?   ▶

HOW CAN I GIVE MY CHILD **ATTENTION** FROM AFAR?

A physically absent parent can still make their presence felt in lots of creative ways. You might leave notes at home telling your child how you feel about them. Avoid phrases like 'I hope you'll be good while I'm away' or 'Take care of Mummy or Daddy for me': these notes should be about giving them attention regardless of how they behave. While you're away, you can make use of FaceTime, Skype, texting or a family Facebook page to keep in touch, sharing pictures of the city or country where you are. Sending postcards and letters is a great way of showing your child the attention you are paying them from afar; many children even like to collect them in a scrapbook. By making these (or similar) gestures, you are demonstrating your attention to and connection with your child—and showing how valuable your child is to you.

CASE STUDY: A mother came to me to seek help for the behaviour of her three-year-old son. She and her husband both worked long days in the city, and were concerned that their son was highly aggressive and attention seeking both at his nursery school and in the evenings at home. When I asked about her evening routine, she revealed that she would catch up on her emails when first getting home. She also admitted to asking about her son's behaviour ('What has gone wrong today?') in front of him whenever she picked him up from school.

The simple change I suggested was for her to finish her emails on the train, then turn off her phone and walk home through the park. This gave her a few minutes to herself, and allowed her to leave work behind. Then, when she arrived home, she was ready to move her attention to her son, and to enjoy hearing about his day in his own words (rather than asking the teacher or nanny about his behaviour). This easy change transformed her son's behaviour both at school and at home.

While these jobs need to be done, think about what small adjustments you can make to your morning or evening schedule to fit in some more downtime with your child. Can things be laid out the night before? Does your child really need to do so many extracurricular activities after school?

Paying attention to a quiet child

It's easy to pay attention to a naturally chatty child (the challenge is to find any peace and quiet!), but it's much

PURESTOCK/THINKSTOCK

3 TIPS FOR THE **RIGHT KIND** OF ATTENTION

1 Try to have a **family meal** at least a couple of times a week where you can give your child positive attention.

2 **Bedtime** can be an invaluable time for giving children one-to-one attention. Try not to be distracted thinking about what you can achieve after your child is asleep. Instead, enjoy reading them their bedtime story or listening to any nighttime worries they may have. This time of day tends to be when children most open up, so take advantage!

3 **Read** to your child, or follow along together with an audiobook. Listening to a story has been found by researchers at Claremont Graduate School to increase our levels of oxytocin: the compassion hormone.

more difficult to show your attention to a quieter, more private child who doesn't seem to want to open up. First, remember that both types of personality are totally normal. Our world tends to value extraverts more—but it's important to allow your introverted child to be themselves.

Avoid the dreaded questions 'How was your day?' or 'What did you do today?'. Unless your child happily chats away in response, you are wasting your breath by pushing it. You are trying to show an interest in your child's life, but after a long day of answering questions

at school, they are more likely to feel put on the spot—especially when expected to deliver a long, satisfactory answer. Instead, you could try a more specific prompt: perhaps asking everyone in the family, including the parents, to share something which made them mad, sad or glad that day. Alternatively, just start talking: sharing stories about your own day can make it easier for your child to chime in with stories of their own—or talking about the news can allow your child to open up about their thoughts without feeling their own privacy is being invaded.

The important thing is that even your most introverted child is given space to talk when they are ready. If you have one child who is much more talkative than the other, you may want to try using a 'talking object': whoever has the object in front of them may take a turn to speak, and adults must follow the rules as well!

Giving attention

Clearly, receiving enough attention is hugely important for a child's emotional wellbeing—but just as important is a child's ability to pay attention to others. Simple acts of paying attention such as volunteering for a charity, expressing gratitude for something, or even smiling ▶

and greeting a passerby have all been suggested to increase wellbeing. This is actually pretty unsurprising: the brain is a very social organ that thrives on emotional connection, and so when we give positive attention to others, our brain releases hormones such as oxytocin, which increase our feelings of trust and safety.

An incredibly useful skill to teach your child is how to give attention to themselves. It may feel strange at first, but teach them to give themselves a hug when they are feeling sad, or at least to ask for one when they notice they need it.

Another aspect of attention-giving is that of being able to direct one's attention to specific objects, people, or experiences. This ability is important for learning, achieving, or developing any type of skill—and for making connections in relationships. Your child will find it much harder to do when they have distractions such as TV on in the background, when they are hungry or when they are tired (something to

be aware of when it's time for them to do their homework). Fitting in some form of movement or exercise can help children discharge energy and prepare to refocus.

Attention difficulties

Make sure that you have age- and gender-appropriate expectations for your child's attention span. In general, boys tend to be about three years behind girls in terms of emotional development, so avoid criticising and comparing an eight-year-old boy with his much more focused five-year-old sister. If you have a summer baby, remember that they are almost a whole year in age behind some of their peers, and may struggle with what is expected of them when they start school. Children are now allowed to begin school outside the school year into which they were born, and this can make a real difference to your child's mental health and wellbeing. Many parents worry about allowing a child to drop a year, but remember, by making this decision you are allowing them to learn and develop at their own pace—

and not according to some arbitrary birth date policy.

If your child consistently struggles to pay attention to a task for more than a few minutes, is easily distracted, and/or finds it difficult to sit for any length of time, it is worth getting an assessment from an educational psychologist, as they may have ADHD (attention deficit hyperactivity disorder). Children with ADHD are often wonderfully outgoing and creative, but will need help and support to thrive in school.

Beware of misdiagnosing ADHD. A struggle to pay attention may be caused by lack of maturity, anxiety, or an undiagnosed mental health problem such as depression. Children need particular help learning to manage difficult emotions, and these issues need to be ruled out first, before a diagnosis of ADHD is confirmed. Don't be hesitant about sharing any parental conflicts or family troubles with the school; schools are used to this and it is important for them to be informed so that they can give your child appropriate support. ∎

AUTHOR'S TIPS

6 WAYS TO TEACH YOUR CHILD TO PAY ATTENTION

1 If your child has had an argument with a friend, encourage them to express their feelings but also to understand that their friend may **see things differently**.

2 Encourage your child to pay attention to those outside the immediate family: for example, **interacting** with baristas, waiters, or shop assistants. For young children, make it clear they mustn't interact too much with strangers when you are not present.

3 Stop and **notice** homeless people that you pass on the street. Charities do not encourage the giving of money,

but perhaps you and your child together could ask a homeless person if you can buy them some food. If your child takes notice of what is happening around them, this will raise their awareness of different world issues.

4 Volunteer as a family, perhaps at Christmas to deliver food packages.

5 Plan and cook a meal together as a family followed by a DVD or board game, with each member of the family taking **responsibility** for a different aspect of the evening.

6 Be a role model: let your child observe you giving your attention to other people.

VOYAGERIX/ISTOCK/THINKSTOCK

WHERE CAN MY CHILD FIND PRIVACY IN OUR SOCIAL WORLD?

We know that humans need intimacy (**see p. 41**), community (**see p. 34**) and attention (**see p. 43**)—but we also have a fundamental need for privacy, which we start developing as young as six to eight years old. By mid-childhood, children need to have private spaces over which they can exert appropriate control, and they may not wish to share all their thoughts and feelings. In our digital and surveillance-driven age, the very concept of privacy is being eroded—so how can we get it back, and why do we need to?

Think about how you behave when you know that nobody is watching. Whether it's singing out loud, dancing round the bedroom or watching a guilty pleasure movie—there are things you do when you're alone that you wouldn't let even your closest friend

see. The same applies to your child: they need time to explore their own personalities away even from the loving eye of a parent. Privacy allows them to be more spontaneous, to explore their emotions without inhibitions, and to be more truly themselves.

Time spent alone (maybe even being bored!) gives children a chance to reflect on and process the events of the day; it is the vital breathing space in the life-long process of self-development.

Introverts and extraverts

Privacy is a core need for all humans, regardless of whether they are more introverted or extraverted (**see p. 39 for more on personality types**). An extraverted child may find it harder to recognise their need for privacy, and indeed, may need less of it, as they ▶

IN THE KNOW

"When privacy and its purportedly outdated values must be balanced against the cutting edge imperatives of national security, efficiency and entrepreneurship, privacy comes up the loser. The list of privacy's counter weights is long and growing. The recent additions of social media, mobile platforms, cloud computing and artificial intelligence-driven data mining now threatens to tip the scale entirely, placing privacy in permanent opposition to the progress of knowledge."
JULIE E. COHEN, LEGAL SCHOLAR. Taken from 'What Privacy Is For', Harvard Law Review (2013)

gain their energy from socialising; however, this doesn't mean they don't need time to themselves to process their busy days. Introverts, on the other hand, will actively crave the time alone; they may enjoy socialising and spending time with their friends, but being alone allows them to 'recharge their batteries' both mentally and physically.

Private hobbies

Spending time alone gives children a chance to pursue the hobbies which will enrich their lives. Of course, many of these pursuits can be great as bonding activities—but it is worth allowing your child to approach these hobbies by themselves as well. Whether it's playing alone with their toys, watching their favourite TV show, getting lost in a book, or kicking a ball around the garden, this alone time will often allow your child to notice more, and to reflect more personally on the experience.

Physical and psychological privacy

There are two types of privacy: physical and psychological. Psychological privacy means the right to keep our thoughts and feelings private, and only share them when we feel comfortable. Physical privacy means ownership over our own bodies, our bedrooms or personal spaces; it requires that nobody is rummaging through our belongings, or reading our diaries. This overlaps in many ways with the need for autonomy and control (see p. 30): even very young children need the opportunity to make small choices of their own, and take on responsibility in their own lives.

Parents often accidentally violate both these types of privacy—by tidying their children's rooms for them, or by sharing stories about funny things their children have said, or difficulties they

5 WAYS TO GIVE YOUR CHILD **PRIVACY**

1 Allow your child to have **personal space**; even if they are sharing a room with a sibling, they will need their own bed, chest of drawers or table, etc. Respect this area as your child's personal space and resist the temptation to rearrange it; family rules about tidiness may still apply, but let your child take responsibility for keeping it organised.

2 Always **knock** before walking in to their room, even if you have a policy against locking doors.

3 Even if you encourage your child to share their **toys**, recognise special attachments they may have to a specific toy. If they feel that one belongs to them, their siblings should ask before playing with it, and should take special care of it.

4 Show an interest in your child's thoughts and feelings, but **don't demand they tell you everything**—and don't take it personally if they keep things to themselves.

5 Don't broadcast your child across your **own social media**. It is tempting to upload cute pictures or funny stories, but remember that your child has a right to their own privacy.

THINKSTOCK

are facing. (Remember that children can often be embarrassed by stories that adults wouldn't consider to be embarrassing; it's worth checking with your child before you publicly tell their stories.)

Children's bodies

Physical touch is very important in the bonding process, and parents naturally love kissing and cuddling their children—but children also need privacy in relation to their bodies.

It is crucial that children are taught from a very young age that they can say 'no' to any touch that makes them feel uncomfortable. They should also know not to keep any inappropriate touching a secret, even when asked to. For them to understand the vital importance of this, the message must not be contradicted by any forced physical touch—even something as seemingly harmless as demanding your child hugs and accepts a kiss from a grandparent. If a child feels

able to say 'no' to a member of their own family, they will be more confident saying 'no' to anyone making them uncomfortable.

Make clear to your child that anything covered by underwear is private. Nobody should ask to see or touch these parts of their body, and if they do, your child should say 'no'. Explain that there may be times when a parent or family member will need to touch these parts to help with washing; a doctor or nurse may also need to see or touch these private parts, but they should always explain why and ask if it is OK first. This explanation and request for permission is key: your child should understand that their body belongs entirely to them and nobody else. No one has the right to make your child do anything with their body that makes them uncomfortable, and if they do, your child should tell an adult they trust.

Private thoughts

You know that it's important ▶

AUTHOR'S TIPS

ISN'T MY CHILD **TOO YOUNG** FOR THESE CONVERSATIONS?

Some parents fear that talking about inappropriate touching may frighten their child and cause them to worry. These conversations shouldn't happen as a one-off, but instead as a way of relating to children in the context of their bodies. Weave these topics throughout everyday discussion: you could try talking about it in the context of someone bullying us into doing something we don't want to do, for example. Demonstrate the importance of respecting other's bodies in your own actions: explaining before you help your child wash their private parts; allowing your child to refuse a cuddle. That way, you will be able to teach your child these crucial lessons without an intense, fear-mongering conversation.

for your child to have intimate relationships (**see p. 41**) and to feel able to share their innermost thoughts and feelings—but sometimes, they need to be able to keep things to themselves. Knowing that they can keep their thoughts private gives them space to daydream without fear of being judged, or to process their emotions about other people without the need for awkward confrontations.

Privacy is also a core element of any relationship. Think about how differently you talk to your child versus your partner, or a family member versus a close friend: even though all of these might be intimate relationships, you will still keep parts of yourself back from each person. Hard as it may be for a parent to accept, your child needs this same privilege: as they grow older, there are certain parts of their personality that they will explore with friends and want to keep private from you.

Secrets

Explain to your child the difference between good secrets and bad secrets. Surprise parties and birthday gifts are good secrets: they are being kept secret only to bring more joy when they are revealed. Adults should never ask a child to keep a secret which worries, scares or upsets them: these are bad secrets. Secrets should never be kept in exchange for something; your child should never feel afraid of telling a secret. Abusers often use phrases such as 'It's our little secret': this makes the child feel they are colluding with the perpetrator and leaves them scared that they will get into trouble for telling. Be careful as a parent not to use this language unthinkingly—and do not ask your child to keep a secret from another parent or loved one, unless you can explain that it's a good secret that will be revealed in the end. Even in the case of good secrets, try not to put too much pressure on your child: they should never get into trouble for telling a secret that was making them feel uneasy. ■

CREATAS IMAGES/THINKSTOCK

HOW MUCH SHOULD I
PRAISE
MY CHILD?

Humans have an emotional need for achievement: to know what we are good at, to set and reach goals, to gain a sense of mastery and competence in a few areas of our lives, to stretch our minds and bodies. Without this sense of achievement, we can become bored and lethargic, and may lose motivation, which in turn might leave us stressed or anxious.

For a long time, parents have been told to heap global praise on their children in an attempt to raise their self-esteem—but this praise is empty, and may actually put pressure on your child. If your child believes you are praising them because they are 'so clever' or 'always do so well in school', they will feel a sense of achievement that is conditional upon them living up to

this. This can lead to low self-worth, or it might encourage them to become too goal-orientated (leaving them stressed whenever a goal is not met).

Your child is far more likely to develop good self-worth if they know exactly what their strengths are, and if the efforts they put into new challenges are acknowledged. If you praise them for working hard to prepare for a test, for example, then they will feel a sense of achievement regardless of the result.

Mistakes and failures

It's easy for children to become afraid of failure, especially when they have always been highly praised for getting things right. Do not encourage this fear: making mistakes and learning from them is actually a vital part of ▶

"We praise our children whenever they give something a go, whether or not it is a success. My daughter recently tried underwater hockey and didn't like it, but I was so pleased with her for trying! We praise them for entering a race, even if they lose. We also praise them when they do something kind. They sometimes play their musical instruments at an older relative's tea party, and we tell them how much it will have meant to that relative that they made the effort—even if they made a few mistakes."

JOANNA, PARENT OF TWO

developing competency and mastery—and it is only by welcoming failure that your child will be able to develop a passion for learning.

Failures can also help your child recognise and accept their weaknesses as well as their strengths, which will allow them to work effectively in a team. And accepting weaknesses doesn't mean they can't strive to improve: in fact, your child should learn to see themselves as a 'work in progress'. (This is something that young children may need help with; they tend to see their abilities as fixed.)

Goal setting

Putting in effort to achieve an explicit goal, whether long or short term, can bring about a great sense of accomplishment and self-worth. Where many people go wrong, however, is in putting the sole importance on the outcome; there is plenty to be gained from the challenge itself. Reviewing and adapting any goals that turned out to be unobtainable should also be encouraged as a worthwhile part of the challenge.

Be careful not to push goals on your child; instead, try to create an atmosphere in which your child is inspired to set their own goals. Let them see you set goals for yourself, and show them how you are trying to achieve them. Encourage curiosity and open-mindedness: regardless of whether or not your child achieves each new thing they attempt, you should praise their willingness to step outside their comfort zone. Notice and describe the smallest efforts and achievements, particularly when your child is very young, and let them know how proud you are of them. Avoid rescuing a child too quickly when they are struggling (and try to manage your frustrations when they take forever to tie their shoelaces while you're trying

IN THE KNOW

"I've seen so many people with this one consuming goal of proving themselves—in the classroom, in their careers and in their relationships. Every situation calls for a confirmation of their intelligence, personality or character. Every situation is evaluated: Will I succeed or fail? Will I look smart or dumb? Will I be accepted or rejected? Will I feel like a winner or loser?"

CAROL DWECK

Taken from Mindset Online

to rush out of the house!).

As your child grows up, they will find their success measured increasingly by concrete achievements: how many marks out of ten in a test; how many A*s at GCSE; how many university offers they receive. Your child will be better equipped to cope with these times of their life if they know how to appreciate and enjoy challenges—and if they have learned not to measure their own worth purely through concrete achievements.

Achieving your best

As inspirational as you may think it sounds, avoid telling your child that sheer motivation and hard work is all it takes to be a Beethoven or an Einstein. Instead, celebrate with your child that their true potential is unknown and unpredictable—and that with a bit of effort and a commitment to facing challenges, they will achieve their personal best! This can be incredibly exciting and liberating, and is a great way to keep your child motivated in the face of failures and rejections.

Avoid praise which is focused on outcomes—such as winning a race, or getting the top result in an exam. Praising these achievements puts value on your child comparing themselves to others, instead of focusing on achieving their own personal best. ∎

TRY PHRASING IT THIS WAY

Avoid: 'This is so much better than the last essay you wrote, which had lots of spelling and grammatical errors in it. This one is much easier to read.'

Instead, say: 'You've worked really hard this term on your spelling. This essay has a lovely flow to it and I really enjoyed reading it. Your descriptions are interesting with very few spelling and grammatical mistakes; it really caught my imagination. How did you feel writing it?'

7 WAYS TO PRAISE YOUR CHILD

1 Praise the **effort** your child put into something, and the skills they utilised.

2 Congratulate your child for their **persistence**, and for managing the frustration they may have felt—but also acknowledge, savour and celebrate the positive emotions experienced along the way.

3 Keep praise **descriptive**, specific and genuine rather than bountiful. Avoid praising your child when they have not put in any real effort: this will devalue the praise you give in the future.

4 Focus your praise on factors within your child's **control**. (Winning a race, for example, depends on other people's performance, which your child cannot control.)

5 Acknowledge progress, but avoid **negative comparisons**. For example, you can praise the effort your child has put into improving their spelling, but should avoid criticising their past mistakes.

6 Affirm **goal-setting**. Even if your child sets themselves an over-enthusiastic goal which they never reach, don't focus on this as a failure. Instead, explore what they learnt from the experience, and praise their positive attitude, and set a new goal.

7 Note that some children prefer to be **praised in private** rather than in public.

HOW CAN MY CHILD FIND THEIR PURPOSE?

A vital aspect of our psychological wellbeing is that we have a sense of meaning and purpose: it is this that gives us our reason to live. What gives our lives meaning is very personal to each of us—but it is likely to include a combination of family, friends, our job or hobbies, and, for some people, our faith or spirituality. Finding our purpose means looking outside ourselves, towards the people we love, towards a community to which we feel we can contribute, or towards a higher power.

When our lives lack meaning, everyday activities start to feel pointless. Children and young people who have no meaning and purpose in their lives are at risk of becoming self-centred, and losing any enthusiasm to engage with life—which in itself can lead to anxiety or depression. It is also important that one's purpose is not derived from a single source: this can lead to narrow-mindedness, and severe stress if the source of that purpose is ever taken away.

It is purpose taken from a variety of factors that keeps us looking forward in life, and motivates us to try new challenges. It is not enough merely to be in pursuit of material wealth: even

4 WAYS TO HELP YOUR CHILD FIND
PURPOSE AND MEANING

AUTHOR'S TIPS

1 Share **your own passions** with your child. This might mean involving them in your hobbies, or it might mean taking them to your workplace and giving them a snapshot of your life. Show them where you derive some of your own meaning and purpose.

2 Notice how your child expresses themselves, and in which situations they are at their most **engaged** and stimulated. Ask them how they feel in these situations, using open-ended questions that elicit more than 'yes' or 'no' answers—and really listen to what they have to say.

3 Give your child the opportunity to try a **variety of experiences:** different sports, musical instruments, art classes or gymnastics, for example. Allow them to choose for themselves which hobbies interest them the most. If they lose interest, do not push them to continue—but explore with them why they wish to stop. After discussing it with you, they may decide by themselves to continue, or you may unearth and solve a specific problem that was standing in the way.

4 Use specific and descriptive praise **(see p. 51)** to encourage your child in their **strengths**.

money becomes meaningless if we do not feel connected to something bigger than ourselves. So how can we help our children find true meaning and purpose in their lives?

Religion or spirituality
People with a religious or spiritual belief often feel like they have more meaning in their lives, as they believe in or worship something greater than themselves. It doesn't necessarily have to include a god or higher power; a spiritual belief might centre around the interconnectedness of people, for example. Any faith your child develops should be positive (not driven by fear of what will happen if they do not believe) and personal; in other words, it should not be imposed on them by their parents or their culture. Introduce your child to a range of belief systems, and allow them to develop their own ideas.

Doing good
Some people find purpose by doing good for others: caring for their friends and family, volunteering for their community, or perhaps seeking jobs that they feel make a real difference to society. Even when your child is young, you can talk about the contributions they can make to their surroundings: perhaps take them volunteering and explain how they are helping people in need, or ask them what differences they would like to make to the world. It can also help to talk about what your child's particular strengths are, and how they might use them.

Education and learning
As our education system becomes more results-focused, children are losing sight of the inherent value of learning. Education should be about far more than the mere acquisition of knowledge: it is also about the sheer joy of learning life skills, values, beliefs and habits. ▶

IN THE KNOW

"Use your signature strengths and virtues in the service of something much larger than you are."

MARTIN SELIGMAN, PSYCHOLOGIST

Ideally, children should have a thirst for knowledge and self-development; they should be inspired to self-direct their learning, and to view being stretched and challenged as positive and constructive. When you talk about education with your child, make an effort to keep the focus away from grades and exams, or even from the specific knowledge they have retained, focusing instead on the joy inherent in learning new things.

Sadly, retaining specific knowledge is how your child will progress successfully through the education system—but when you are not helping them revise for formal exams, you can help them learn in a much broader way.

By holding discussions, posing and encouraging questions, and exploring books, films and museums together, you can inspire your child to love finding out about the world in which they live. Young people who develop this passion for learning will be better able to make informed judgements, and to develop their own moral system to guide and support them through their lives. These values, and the ability to draw their own conclusions, will contribute greatly to your child's sense of meaning and purpose. ∎

TRY PHRASING IT THIS WAY

Try asking your child some of these questions:

- What do you enjoy doing most?

- How do you feel about yourself when you're doing that?

- What is important to you?

- What makes you feel good about yourself?

- Who do you look up to, and why?

- What would you like to do when you're older?

Parents

Raising an emotionally healthy child is no easy task: you will need to manage your own stresses and frustrations in order to take on the job. It is crucial, therefore, that you are properly looking after your own emotional wellbeing during the challenge of being a parent.

NADOPHOTOS/ISTOCK/THINKSTOCK

PAY YOURSELF SOME ATTENTION

Take some time for yourself, during which you do not need to be meeting the needs of anyone else. Go for a walk, read a book, take a bath or just sit quietly with a cup of tea: what is key is that you will be paying yourself some much-deserved attention, and allowing yourself some time to explore your private thoughts and feelings.

ASK YOURSELF...

How am I taking care of myself right now? What do I need to nourish me?

ASK YOURSELF...

Do I derive my purpose in life from more than one source? Make sure it's not just wrapped in one thing, such as being a parent; when your child leaves home, this can leave you feeling unfulfilled.

BE PROUD OF YOURSELF

Acknowledge your own strengths and achievements, and allow yourself to feel a sense of satisfaction and contentment at knowing you have done a job well. Remember to take pride in your efforts, too: you are trying your hardest to be a good friend; you are doing your best at your job; you are parenting as well as you can. Don't berate yourself for any failures; instead, let your child see you congratulate yourself for each new thing you have tried, no matter the outcome.

SOCIALISE

You need people in your life who take an interest in you as a person—not just as a parent or partner. Spend time with your partner or intimate friends away from your child—giving you a chance to appreciate each other in a wider context. Don't rely on your relationship with your child, no matter how close it is, to fulfil all your emotional needs.

Make an effort to give attention to those outside your immediate circle: the barista at your coffee shop, perhaps, or the school receptionist. This will give you a wider sense of community.

WHAT INNER RESOURCES DOES MY CHILD HAVE?

Your child's physical and emotional needs are varied and complex, and it can seem like an impossible task to keep them fulfilled. Thankfully, it's not all up to you: your child has all kinds of inherent emotional resources that can help them sustain high levels of wellbeing. Helping your child cultivate these inner resources is one of the greatest gifts you can give as a parent.

Emotions are important

It's crucial to remember that all emotions are important, even the ones we don't like. It might be nicer to experience joy, love and excitement— but we all need to feel anger, sadness and worry sometimes too.

Be careful not to punish your child for expressing what we often call negative emotions, especially when they are very young and only just learning how to process them. Children can play up because they are confused, frustrated or hurt and they don't have the language to express this. These emotions are important, and you don't want to discourage your child from communicating them— otherwise they may end up trying to repress them. For your child to face life's challenges, they need to develop emotional intelligence—and this means

4 WAYS TO TEACH YOUR CHILD ABOUT EMOTION

1 Express **your own emotions** to your child throughout the day. Talk openly about the 'negative' emotions as well as the positive ones, without showing disdain for either.

2 **Name the emotions** that your child is experiencing ('You seem sad'), to help them develop a vocabulary for their feelings.

3 **Acknowledge difficult feelings,** even if they lead to bad behaviour. ('I appreciate that you are upset with your brother, but you mustn't hit him.') Make sure your child knows you are challenging the inappropriate expression of the feeling, but never the feeling itself.

4 Read **story books** together and talk to your child about the emotions involved. Ask if they can work out how a character might be feeling, and ask if they have ever felt something similar, what made them feel like that, and how they could express that feeling in a positive or helpful way. (**For more exercises like this, see p. 61 on empathy.**)

JUPITERIMAGES/PHOTOS.COM/THINKSTOCK

being able to identify, appreciate and communicate the myriad of emotions they might experience in any given day.

Managing emotions

Emotions are important, but when we become overwhelmed by them, we stop being able to act rationally. Being emotionally aroused actually stops the prefrontal cortex (the part of the brain in charge of rational thinking) from functioning coherently, and so we are unable to have useful discussions.

The first step towards managing emotions is acknowledging them. Children who are told never to be angry, for example, may end up flooded with anger and unable to process it. If, on the other hand, they are able to recognise and appreciate that they feel angry, they can learn calmly to manage the emotion.

Create a feelings space in your house where anyone can go for a few moments alone when they're angry or sad. This is not a 'naughty step'; you never want your child to feel punished for processing their emotions. Let your child see you visiting the feelings space so they feel encouraged to use it themselves. Allow them to use the feelings space privately, but you might ▶

suggest that they use it to take slow steady breaths and to give themselves a hug. Let them know they can ask for a hug too if that's what they need!

If your child is playing up, gently suggest that they spend some time in the feelings space allowing the emotion to pass or settle. Once they have calmed down, talk through what they were feeling, and how they could have expressed it differently. Don't dwell too long on this, though, unless your child wants to: you want your child to understand that sometimes mistakes happen and that it can be easy to move on.

Cultivating positive emotions

Our brains are like Velcro for negative emotions and Teflon for positive. You will have noticed this yourself: when receiving feedback from friends or colleagues, you tend to focus on the one negative comment, even amongst an abundance of positive ones. Luckily, the brain isn't a fixed organ: we can literally change it by the way we think and behave.

Learning actively to cultivate positive emotions (rather than just experiencing fewer negative ones) can give your

wellbeing a serious boost: it can help people recover faster from depression, manage their stress and develop greater resilience. Positive emotions have also been shown to improve personal relationships and one's ability to express gratitude; they have even been shown to have a positive effect on one's immune system.

As adults, it takes a bit of work to retrain our brains to do this, but for children, it can be much easier. The

brain picks up strong habits: if your child learns early on how to nurture positive emotions, then this habit will stick with them. Teach your child how to notice and savour the good moments in their day-to-day life, acknowledging the thoughts, feelings and bodily sensations that accompany these moments (but not trying to analyse them). Even 30 seconds spent savouring a positive emotion will create a memory of that emotion within the brain; each time your child does this, that memory will become stronger and more lasting. Eventually, experiencing and savouring positive emotions will become a habit. ■

CASE STUDY: Two groups of students were set a puzzle: they had to draw a line to help a mouse find its way out of a maze. One group of students were shown a piece of cheese at the exit (a positive, approach-orientated puzzle), while the second group were shown an owl inside the maze which the mouse needed to escape (a negative, avoidance-orientated puzzle). Both sets of students completed the puzzles in about two minutes; what was fascinating was what happened next. The students were then asked to complete an unrelated task which measured creativity. Students who had helped the mouse find the cheese, and had their approach pathways triggered, were twice as creative as those who had helped the mouse escape the owl, which activated the avoidance pathway in their brain.

THIS MIGHT HELP

Barbara Fredrickson's book **Positivity** gives a thorough explanation of how cultivating positive emotions can build optimism, resilience, openness and an acceptance towards oneself, as well as having positive effects on one's physical health.

ANTONIOGUILLEM/ISTOCK/THINKSTOCK

HOW CAN I CULTIVATE
EMPATHY IN MY CHILD?

One skill that you can help your child develop is that of empathy: the ability to imagine how someone else is feeling in a particular situation. Empathy is an innate resource in humans, but it still needs cultivating before we are able to use it properly.

Being able to empathise will help your child build intimate relationships, fit into a community, and even find a sense of purpose in their life.

Developing empathy

Empathy can only begin to develop once your child is able to recognise themselves as an individual. Before that point, children literally do not have the capability to empathise—which is why parenting young children, who will not understand that you might be tired or busy, can be so exhausting!

Once your child understands themselves as an individual, they will be able to start recognising and identifying the common feelings we all experience: anger, joy, sadness, disgust, fear, etc.

Next, they will learn to appreciate that others experience different thoughts and feelings than they do. This is empathy.

Empathy and community

Encouraging your child to interact with their community (see p. 34) is a great way of showing them that the world does not revolve around them. At home, this might mean sharing out the chores between each family member, and explaining to your child how it helps you when they pitch in.

When going through school reports with your child, give as much praise to comments related to community involvement as you do to academic achievements. If this isn't discussed in the school report, you could ask your child's teacher at parents' evenings if your child has been joining in.

It is also important that your child can empathise with those outside their inner circle; with people that they ▶

5 WAYS TO CULTIVATE **EMPATHY** IN YOUR CHILD

1 Show your child that you **understand and appreciate their feelings,** whether or not you agree with them. Even if your child is lashing out and acting inappropriately, acknowledge the emotions that are driving this behaviour.

2 Ask your child if they can **work out how people are feeling** in different situations. If somebody cuts in front of you in the car, for example, you might ask them if they know how it made you feel, or if they can work it out from your facial expression. You could even play a game where one person acts out an emotion and the other guesses what it is.

3 Hold **family discussions** related to topical news items, reflecting on how each person in the situation may have been feeling. Explore ethical dilemmas, either from the news or from situations that you or your child have found yourselves in.

4 **Allow everyone to share their thoughts** after any family conflict. Take turns talking, and really listen to whoever is speaking, valuing their feelings even if you think they're wrong or unfair. Encourage each family member to take responsibility for having hurt someone else's feelings, and to apologise for it—but make it clear that you appreciate it was a mistake. Do remember that some people need time and space to process their thoughts before talking them through.

5 **Demonstrate** empathy yourself. Let your child observe you behaving empathetically towards them and others. Point out when others are demonstrating strong empathy.

might never actually meet. Choose a charity to support and explain how it helps people whose lives might be vastly different from your child's. You might suggest your child donates some of their own pocket money (though let them make this choice themselves)—or you might want to volunteer as a family.

Empathy and intimacy

Your child will need good skills of empathy if they are to develop strong intimate relationships. You can help them develop these in the way you talk about any conflicts they have with their friends. If your child is upset about an argument they have had, empathise with their emotions, and take care not to dismiss their feelings. However, don't blindly take their side: point out how the other person might have felt—and if your child may have contributed to the situation.

In the end, you want your child to feel loved no matter what they have done—but you also want them to take responsibility for their behaviour and appreciate how they might have made somebody else feel. ■

TRY PHRASING IT THIS WAY

AVOID: 'You shouldn't have done that.'

INSTEAD, TRY: 'I wonder how Hannah might have felt when that happened?'

AVOID: 'You must have done something horrible for Hannah to get so cross with you.'

INSTEAD, TRY: 'I wonder if anything you said made Hannah feel upset. Can you think of anything that might have hurt her feelings?'

HOW CAN I RAISE A
COMPASSIONATE
CHILD?

Compassion is the desire to relieve the suffering of another person; the word literally means 'to suffer together'. It is not the same as empathy (see p. 61), which is the ability to understand another's emotions: one could use this empathetic knowledge in order to manipulate or hurt somebody, which would not be compassionate at all. However, the two are closely related: when we feel compassion, we release the hormone oxytocin, which triggers the part of our brain associated with empathy.

Using empathy and compassion together is the foundation of intimate, caring relationships (see p. 41)—and we should direct both these tools towards ourselves, as well.

Developing compassion
Much like empathy, the ability to be compassionate is a resource innate to most humans—but it needs cultivating in order to be truly beneficial to our wellbeing.

Compassion is born from a sense of common humanity. Talk to your child about the struggles that all humans have: their friends, other children at school, and children all over the world leading vastly different lives. Tell them some of your own childhood stories that they can relate to. Your child needs to understand that we are all humans with the ability to feel pain and sadness— this is empathy—but it is once they feel a sense of connection and shared humanity that they will begin to feel compassionate.

When your child is sad, even something as simple as a hug or a soothing touch from you can feel very comforting to them. You might also ask them what you can do to make them feel better; this will get them thinking about how humans can help take away some of each other's pain. Kindness is a very undervalued virtue in our society, so it is worth emphasising to your child quite how important you think it really is; a lot of this emphasis will come from your own kind behaviour towards them and others.

Be careful, however, not to push your child reluctantly into acts of kindness. It might be clear to you that the child being mean to them at school needs a ▶

4 WAYS TO TEACH YOUR CHILD **COMPASSION**

1 As a family, challenge each other to do **one act of kindness every day**: whether it's as small as a smile, or whether it's asking somebody who looks left out at school if they'd like to join in with a game.

2 Give your child a small amount of money, and ask them to come up with **creative ideas** about how they could use it to do something kind. You could also set aside money as a family, and brainstorm together how you are going to use it to help others.

3 **Volunteer** as a family: helping out with local agencies, delivering parcels at Christmas, or perhaps working on a nature conservation project. Talk about how your actions will have helped somebody else feel happier.

4 Encourage your child to write **thank you** notes, not just for presents, but whenever someone has done something kind or thoughtful for them. **(See p. 66 for more on gratitude.)**

friend, but forcing your child to invite them over to your house will only make your child feel resentful, and that you are not listening to their feelings. Instead, there's something easier you can do: teach your child to silently wish them well. Do this every time you see or hear about somebody who might be suffering: together with your child, send them your best wishes. Once your child has learned to genuinely wish happiness upon others, even those people they don't particularly get on with, they will be inspired to take kind action of their own volition.

Self-compassion

Self-compassion is one of the key resources with which you can equip your child. It will allow your child to comfort and soothe themselves through times of challenge and pain, so you know that they will cope even when you can't be there to help them.

Some people confuse self-compassion with self-pity, which is disempowering and emotionally draining. They worry that a self-compassionate child will stop working on certain areas of their lives or trying to improve—but this is untrue.

THINKSTOCK

Those who show greater compassion to themselves and others often find the following benefits:

• **Higher resilience to stress due to the lowering of stress hormones**

• **Greater ability to take pleasure in things, leading to an increase in happiness**

• **A more optimistic outlook, and an unlikeliness to worry about things that might go wrong in the future**

• **Improved relationships with partners, family and friends**

MERZZIE/ISTOCK/THINKSTOCK

Self-compassion means treating yourself in the same way you would treat a dear and treasured friend: you would show them support and empathy even if they had done something wrong; you would allow them to feel sad and cry if they needed; you would accept that their flaws are part of what makes them human—but you would also encourage them to make changes and help them put their problems into perspective.

Teaching your child self-compassion will help them evaluate themselves honestly without judgement, and work on their flaws without becoming self-deprecating. Harsh self-criticism shuts down creative thinking; self-compassion allows your child to stand back and reflect on a situation productively.

One really simple way for your child to show themselves compassion is to give themselves a hug (or, if this feels awkward, simply to place their hand over their heart), and to say to themselves some words of reassurance. The comforting touch will actually activate the soothing oxytocin hormone.

Self-esteem

Self-compassion is not the same as self-esteem. For the last few decades, psychologists have encouraged parents to build the self-esteem of their

IN THE KNOW

"Instead of mercilessly judging and criticising yourself for various inadequacies or shortcomings, self-compassion means you are kind and understanding when confronted with personal failings—after all, who ever said you were supposed to be perfect?"

DR. KRISTIN NEFF
Self-Compassion.org

children—but is this the right approach? Raising one's self-esteem can often rely on comparisons with one's peers in order to feel special and superior: it can become unhealthily focused on achievements (**see p. 51**), and it can even result in putting other people down.

Despite the stereotype to the contrary, research from the Simon Fraser University tells us that bullies often have rather high self-esteem, and believe themselves to be better than the people they pick on. (Their emotional wellbeing, on the other hand, is probably rather low!) ■

THIS MIGHT HELP

Self-Compassion: The Proven Power of Being Kind to Yourself by Kristin Neff

The Mindful Path to Self-Compassion by Chris Germer

WHY IS BEING GRATEFUL SO GOOD FOR US?

As humans, we have a tendency to dwell on what is going wrong, and miss out on all the wonderful things happening to us.

When we are experiencing or expressing gratitude, we are looking outside ourselves and acknowledging what is good in the world. Gratitude reminds us to appreciate the other people in our lives, or the opportunities that we have; those who take time to feel grateful for these things generally have much higher wellbeing.

Gratitude and children

Research carried out at the University of Berkeley has suggested that the emotional benefits of expressing gratitude may only kick in upon reaching adulthood. Children and adolescents benefit from being thanked, but not necessarily from giving thanks—unlike adults. However, gratitude is a difficult habit to pick up as an adult, so it is worth developing your child's skills of gratitude at a young age so that they can reap the

benefits later in life.

Gratitude exercises can also help your child become more aware of the world around them—which will have fantastic effects on their wellbeing at any age.

Cultivating gratitude

Taking time to express gratitude can feel like a strange and slightly forced experience to begin with—but as with any new skill, it will feel natural with time.

First, your child needs to learn to

5 GRATITUDE EXERCISES
FOR YOUR CHILD TO TRY

1 Several times a week, get them to **write down** three things, big or small, for which they are grateful. Ask them to notice how each thing makes them feel—not analysing it, but merely experiencing the emotions.

2 Encourage your child to write **thank you notes** to people they appreciate, or to pay them a visit with a home-made cake, card or a bunch of flowers. Encourage spontaneity and creativity here.

3 Challenge your child to give **specific reasons** when they thank people—even baristas, waitresses or hairdressers, for example. This will get them thinking about what they particularly enjoyed about each experience.

4 Remind your child to give **compliments**. This will encourage them to take notice of the people around them.

5 Show **gratitude** for your food. Talk about where the food came from: who has grown it, harvested it and packaged it? How many people were involved in this process? Think about the country and community from which it originated, and how different their lives might be to yours.

perhaps at the end of the day before they fall asleep. It might only take 30 seconds, and is a lovely bedtime routine.

Let your child see you express gratitude yourself towards people you come across in shops or restaurants. Talk to your child about the gratitude you feel towards people who support your community—such as dustbin collectors or street cleaners. Expressing gratitude to other people requires your child to engage with their community (**see p. 34**), and will give them an incredible sense of connection. ■

look outwards and notice what is going on in the world—even very simple things like the sun shining in the morning, or the taste of their cereal at breakfast. When your child has a happy experience, encourage them to notice and savour their emotions. It's a great idea to try mindfulness exercises (**see p. 90**) with your child to help them focus on the here and now, and get out of their own heads.

You can then encourage your child to reflect privately on special moments,

Parents

It's a lot harder to change your emotional habits as an adult—but it's certainly possible. Incorporating just a few positive psychology practices into your daily routine can make an enormous difference to your wellbeing—and it can even help you better engage with the wonderfully fulfilling and challenging job of being a parent.

THINKSTOCK

YOU'RE A GREAT PARENT

Even if you've been tired lately, even if you lost your temper with your child, or were late to pick them up from school—you're a great parent. Have some compassion for yourself: put your hand over your heart and remind yourself this job is difficult, and we all struggle sometimes. Remember, being compassionate means never comparing yourself to others—even favourably! Don't be critical of other parents you know: you're all doing your best.

JUST BREATHE

Even the busiest parent can find two minutes for a breathing exercise—and the boost it will give you will be well worth it. Sit comfortably in a chair, close your eyes, and bring your attention to the sensation of your breath. You do not need to change your breathing rhythm in any way; merely notice it as it flows in and out of your body. As you breathe in, imagine you are breathing in compassion for yourself—and as you breathe out, imagine you are breathing compassion towards someone you love. Notice the sense of warmth and connection you will feel.

SAY THANK YOU

Express gratitude out loud whenever you feel it: towards your child, your partner, even towards total strangers. When you take time to express this, not only will you feel more positive emotions towards those around you, but you will also feel more able to express any concerns you may have.

ASK YOURSELF...

How can I be kind to myself today? Perhaps with a bath, a cup of tea or ten minutes curled up with a book.

HOW CAN I HELP MY CHILD THROUGH DIFFICULT TIMES?

Children will face a variety of issues as they travel through childhood; parents cannot, and should not, protect them from everything. Bumps in the road are a normal and natural part of childhood and family life—but what parents can do is to support their child throughout.

Your child will face hardships throughout their life; your aim is that they will be able to navigate these hard times in the future when you're not there to help them. Protecting them from any painful experiences won't equip your child properly to look after themselves, but nor will standing back in the hope it will 'toughen them up' to be exposed to difficulties. What is needed is balance: a variety of life experiences, each approached with support, love and guidance.

When your child goes through a difficult time, think about which of their emotional or physical needs are not being met, and how you can help make up for this. For example, if you and your partner are separating, your child's need for security may be under threat: think about how you can make them feel more secure in other ways. Remember that children are unique individuals, not carbon copies of parents or siblings. Your child may be naturally more or less resilient than you expect; they may be more or less able to cope with change. Therefore, instead of trying to manage their experience, check in with how well they feel their needs are being met. ▶

PIXELHEADPHOTO/ISTOCK/THINKSTOCK

Resilience

Resilience is the ability to bounce back following adversity, or the ability to persevere, bend and adapt during challenging times rather than collapse or give up. It is not the same as grit, or 'toughing it out'; resilience does not mean that an individual will not experience difficulties, but rather that they will be able to manage their experience during these challenging times. Resilience is now recognised as a key and important element in our wellbeing, and a vital skill to develop within ourselves and our children.

Some children will be more predisposed to be resilient, but you can cultivate resilience in your child through your approach to parenting. The most important thing is to provide a stable and loving environment, in which your child is set high (but

> **Taking care of your child's physical needs is crucial during difficult times. Exercise can be particularly beneficial to a child who is feeling stressed or sad.**

6 WAYS TO HELP YOUR CHILD THROUGH **HARD TIMES**

1 **Talk to them** about how they are feeling. If they are too young, or are otherwise finding it hard to express their feelings in words, they might like to draw a picture or write a story. Acknowledge your child's feelings: don't try to gloss over or deny them.

2 Give your child **time** to work things out—and don't expect them to keep pace with your own emotions.

3 Reassure them that whatever has happened is **not their fault**. Young children in particular may feel they did something wrong to cause their parents to split up, for example. Even older children may blame themselves for certain issues, like getting bullied.

4 Keep your child's school or carers **informed** so that they can be supportive, and look out for any signs of your child not coping.

5 **Be honest** with your child. Children are perceptive and will know something is wrong: if you try to shield them, they may end up feeling uncertain and insecure.

6 As far as possible, **let life continue as normal**. Your routine is bound to change to an extent, and your child may need a little more attention, but try to maintain some normality. This will make your child feel secure, and show them that whatever happens, life can go on.

RSOKOLOFF/ISTOCK/THINKSTOCK

achievable) standards of behaviour and is expected to contribute to family life in a variety of ways (**see p. 27**). Praising your child for their efforts rather than their achievements (**see p. 51**) will also help your child develop resilience in the face of challenges.

Resilient children still experience pain and other difficult emotions, but as they grow and mature, they come to understand these feelings to be temporary, and are not afraid of them. You can encourage this by acknowledging and validating negative emotions whenever they arise, and showing compassion. However, you should not jump in and try to solve your child's problems, as this suggests that their difficult emotions are something from which they ▶

THIS MIGHT HELP

The film **Inside Out** depicts the emotions inside a child's mind, and how they each play a vital role—even sadness.

The book **The Boy Who Didn't Want to Be Sad** is an excellent exploration of the good that sadness brings to our lives.

There are a few signs you can look for that your child is struggling and needs extra support:

- They've developed separation anxiety.
- They're having difficulty concentrating.
- They're having sleep difficulties—either trouble getting to sleep, waking during the night, restless nights or nightmares.
- They seem scared to go to school.
- They've lost their appetite.
- They're acting in an uncharacteristically irritable way, having irrational outbursts, or reverting to behaviour you'd typically expect from a younger child.
- Their behaviour has changed—perhaps withdrawing from activities they used to enjoy.
- They cry for no apparent reason.
- They're complaining of stomach or headaches, or are generally feeling unwell.

need shielding. Instead, encourage them to explore their options, with gentle guidance from you rather than direct advice. Praise your child for taking decisive actions to solve their problems, even if they turn out not to have been the correct solution.

Help your child come to terms with situations that they can't change, rather than trying to deal with the problems yourself (unless you think the problem is severe). Your child will become much more resilient if they are able to accept situations that didn't work out how they hoped. ■

TRY PHRASING IT THIS WAY

AVOID: 'I'm so proud of you for staying happy through this difficult time.' This suggests that happiness is the correct emotion for them to feel, and that they would fail if they were to feel sad.

INSTEAD, TRY: 'This has been a difficult time for you, and you've done really well not to give up even when it must have felt really hard.' This acknowledges that they will have felt a range of emotions, and praises their efforts rather than achievements.

HOW CAN I HELP MY CHILD COPE WITH CHANGE?

How your child responds to change will depend on their personality: some children thrive on change; for others it can be frightening. It can also depend on how many changes are happening at once. Stay tuned in to how your child is coping—and respect any emotions they are feeling. Children who are acting up are probably feeling a lack of security (see p. 27). Make them feel secure in other ways (even if that is just by reassuring them verbally that they are safe) throughout the upheaval of their usual routines.

Be aware that changes such as moving house can be far more unsettling for children than adults, as they have had no control (see p. 30) over the decision-making process. Try to involve your child in big decisions: even if you feel they are too young to have an input, keep them informed along the way—so that by the time the decision is made, they understand it.

Moving house

Leaving a childhood home can be daunting, but moving can actually be a very exciting experience for children. Bring them to visit the new house if possible, or show them pictures. Perhaps you might let them choose their own room, or think about what activities they could do in the new garden, for example.

If you are moving house because of a divorce or separation (see p. 76), remember that there will be other emotions affecting your child. Their upset about moving house may, at least in part, be misplaced sadness from the separation; address both issues separately with your child.

Birth of a new sibling

The birth of a new sibling is exciting for the whole family—but don't underestimate how much it will change your family dynamics. An only child will have to adjust to sharing their parents; a youngest child may suddenly be treated differently as a middle child. How a child responds to this change will depend on how prepared they are: before the birth of a new sibling, talk through in detail with your child what this will mean for your everyday family life.

Don't expect too much from your

child, but don't leave them out either; they may enjoy helping out with the new baby—but protect your one-on-one time with them as well.

Older sibling moving into the adolescent years

A change occurs for a younger child when their older sibling loses interest in the games they used to play together, or even in spending time with their younger sibling at all. It can also be a big change when an older sibling leaves home for boarding school or university. Be ready to step in to fill the older sibling's place if your child asks.

Moving school

Change will occur throughout your child's education: moving from nursery school to junior school to senior school. Depending on your child, these changes may be exciting or frightening; keep an eye out for how your child is reacting. Some changes may seem more negative: perhaps if you have had to move house (and therefore school) due to a separation, or perhaps if you have had to move your child from a fee-paying school because you can no longer afford it. In cases like these it is important to acknowledge the difficult emotions, while encouraging your child to see the positive opportunities.

Staff or carers moving on

Many parents may not appreciate that an au pair or nanny moving on can be unsettling for a child—or perhaps a cleaner or gardener that your child would see regularly. These changes need to be acknowledged, and your child should be given warning. Even if the carer is leaving for negative reasons (perhaps you think they were not fulfilling their role), recognise that your child may have developed a connection with them.

/JUPITERIMAGES/LIQUID LIBRARY/THINKSTOCK

Explain to your child why the person is moving on; if appropriate, the carer can tell your child themselves. Allow them to say goodbye, perhaps with a farewell ritual such as a meal or an outing. Before the carer leaves, your child may like to create a memory box, scrapbook or video. These could be added to a bigger collage of family memories, which they can keep throughout their childhood to remember everyone who played a part in their family community.

As a parent, it is sometimes challenging to acknowledge that your child has a strong attachment to a carer; it may be wrapped up in a sense of guilt as a working parent, leaving you reluctant to admit how important these other individuals are. Try to leave these feelings behind: they are unnecessarily harsh on you. Having a wider community to support you in your role as parent is actually hugely beneficial for your child (see p. 34 for more on community). ■

HOW SHOULD WE TALK TO OUR CHILD ABOUT OUR SEPARATION?

When you have children, divorce or separation no longer just affects you. Even if the person from whom you are separating is not your child's parent, your child will still feel the effects, and suffer a loss of the family unit with which they are familiar. Don't let that make you feel hesitant or guilty about your decision: if a relationship is not working, you need to look after your own needs and make a change—and besides, it may be that a separation actually comes as a relief to a child if the relationship has been unstable. That said, you do need to consider how your divorce or separation will affect your child—and think about how you can support them through the experience.

How to argue

There's nothing inherently wrong with children witnessing conflict; this is part of family life. However, be careful how you argue with your partner in front of your child. You don't want them to overhear constant arguments, or for there to be a high level of unresolved conflict. Be especially careful that your arguments do not

THIS MIGHT HELP

The company Relate provides counselling for families, children and young people.

Never make a child take sides

Respect your child's relationship with your ex. Children are aware that they are made from both of their parents, so they may feel personally attacked by any criticism of their other parent—or towards an ex who played a significant role in raising them. You may be feeling a lot of pain, grief and anger towards your ex—but your child needs to be allowed to direct their own feelings and emotions towards that person, and you should listen to what these feelings are.

If you believe your ex is unsafe to be around your child, this is something you will need to make clear to your child—but explain that they can still love them even while acknowledging that their behaviour is unacceptable.

Keep in touch

You and your partner may no longer be in a relationship, but you are still both an important part of your child's life, particularly if you are both their parents. It is important for your child's ▶

become personal and insulting; try to debate rationally rather than launching into an attack.

If appropriate, explain to your child what the conflict is about, taking care to present both sides of the argument fairly. If your child understands why you and your partner are arguing, the conflict will be less threatening and unsettling to them.

CASE STUDY: I met with an 11-year-old girl who was experiencing sleepless nights, having behaviour problems at school, and becoming withdrawn. Her parents were separating, but her mother was adamant that the girl had no idea. Within minutes of my first session with the girl, she talked about her parents being unhappy, and said that she was worried about them. Upon feeding this back to the parents, they agreed it was time to tell her about the separation. At our second appointment, the girl was very sad about her parents splitting up, but she was relieved to have had her worries discussed—including her worry that she wouldn't see her father after he moved out.

CATHERINE YEULET/ISTOCK/THINKSTOCK

sense of security (see p. 27) that they feel both parents are still there for them—and that means you and your ex need to work together in your child's best interests.

If talking face-to-face with your ex is hard for you, then find another way of communication, perhaps via telephone or email. You can be open with your child about why you are finding it difficult to see your ex (being careful not to be too critical of them), but reassure them that the two of you will continue your roles as parents. This means continuing to make decisions together, maintaining the same rules regarding behaviour and following through on routines.

If you are the parent who has moved out, it is tempting to spoil your child and relax boundaries during the precious times you have together. Try not to do this too much: while your routine is bound to change to some extent, children still want to know where they stand. They may well take advantage if they feel one parent is less strict and you may find that you enjoy that role—but it is not beneficial for your child's sense of security. ∎

"My ex and I took the position of asking ourselves what would be best for the children—and as time went on, for me (and I'm sure for him) that has helped us to chart a course through all the unexpected challenges of life. When the kids are with me, my ex comes to see them regularly after work, and vice versa. We occasionally do day trips together, and if the other one makes a decision that we disagree with, we mostly bite our tongues. It's not a perfect solution by any means—the issues that drove us apart still loom large—but when I put the children at the centre of that picture, it changes the perspective. Those issues become so much less important than ensuring our children have love, stability and security with both their parents."

MOTHER OF TWO, FOLLOWING SEPARATION TWO YEARS AGO

AUTHOR'S TIPS

HOW TO **HELP YOUR CHILD** THROUGH YOUR SEPARATION

DO

• Give them privacy when talking to their other parent on the telephone, or time alone with their other parent in person (unless you feel this is actually unsafe).

• Be open and honest (as far as is age-appropriate) with your child about what is happening.

• Listen to your child about how they are feeling, and let them express their emotions about your ex, or perhaps your ex's new partner, without guilt.

DON'T

• Interrogate your child about how they spent their time with your ex or what they talked about.

• Use your child as a messenger between you and your ex.

• Ask your child to lie to or keep secrets from your ex.

• Tell your child how to feel about the situation or any of the people involved.

HOW CAN I
HELP MY CHILD UNDERSTAND
ILLNESS
AND DEATH?

MONKEYBUSINESSIMAGES/ISTOCK/THINKSTOCK

Coming to terms with the death of a loved one is a painful process for people of all ages, let alone children. Whether it is a relative, a friend or even a pet that they have lost, your child will need support as they travel through the journey of their grief.

Parents often wish to shield their children from the pain of loss and grief, but this approach is not helpful to the development of their emotional intelligence.

Talking to your child

When someone is ill or dying, it is important to let your child be part of what is happening. They will be aware if something is wrong, and it is better for them to hear the truth from you than to fear the worst by themselves.

4 THINGS TO DO BEFORE A HOSPITAL VISIT

1 Prepare your child for what they will see and hear at the hospital. The hospital can advise you on this; you might even ask if a nurse or doctor is willing to talk to your child first.

2 Describe to your child the condition and appearance of the ill person they are visiting.

3 Do some **research** on the hospital equipment being used and how it is helping, and explain this to your child in advance. This can bring a real sense of positivity: 'how amazing is this technology?'

4 Reassure them that most hospital patients do get well. Even if the person you are visiting is terminally ill, this will still be comforting for a child who might otherwise become overwhelmed by the number of other ill people they see on their trip.

> "As a family we had several pets throughout the children's childhood, they took care of them and experienced loss when they died, but organised the funeral and it enabled the conversation of death to be part of family life."
>
> PETER, FATHER OF TWO

It may be sensible, however, to shield your child from some unnecessary worries. You may decide, for example, not to tell your child about any initial medical tests. Once the situation is made clearer it might be a better time to give them some information. Depending on their age, their personality, how noticeable the condition is and what type of treatment is required, you will be able to decide how much information is appropriate to give them—but remain open to answering any further questions they may have, even if your honest answer is that you don't know.

To make sure your child has properly understood what you've told them, ask them to repeat back what you've said in their own words. Children can often misinterpret things and end up unnecessarily frightened.

Always let your child express their own feelings. They will be better able to cope with death and illness if they can process their thoughts about it—and allowing them to communicate their thoughts to you is a large part of that.

It can also be helpful if you convey your own emotions to them: letting them know you are feeling sad can help them address their own feelings. Where possible, however, avoid letting your child see you in particular distress as this may frighten them. Of course, you have needs as well, so don't forcefully repress your own grief to avoid this—but do reassure your child by explaining your emotions to them.

Visiting an ill person

Hospitals increasingly allow visitors, and where possible, taking your child to visit an ill or dying loved one can be a very positive experience. Contact with an ill person can help diminish the mystery of illness and death for your child, and reduce the loneliness that can be felt by both the ill person and their relatives. Bringing a moment of happiness to an ill or dying individual might help your child feel less helpless.

Paying a visit to an ill loved one can encourage your child to open up and ask questions; open avenues of communication are vital in helping your child through this difficult time. It can also help your child develop realistic coping methods.

If hospital visits are not allowed or feasible, your child might like to make a phone call to their ill loved one. Alternatively, if the ill person is not well enough for a phone call, your child could send in a card, letter or gift. Give your child some choice about how they would like to send their best wishes, and how they feel they can provide the most positive help.

Breaking bad news

It is never easy to break the news of a death to a child. The news should come from somebody known to and trusted by the child, using soothing touch if appropriate to comfort and console them.

Let your child know the news as soon as possible, and explain to them exactly what happened, as far as you feel is age-appropriate. If they are not told, they may be left confused or frightened, perhaps imagining something worse than the reality. ▶

TRY PHRASING IT THIS WAY

AVOID: 'They have gone away/to Heaven.' This may leave your child unsettled whenever another of their loved ones goes on a trip—and it might deprive them of closure if they believe the dead person is coming back.

Instead, explain the facts of their death, and then, if it is part of your belief system, reassure your child that the dead person's soul has gone on to another place.

AVOID: 'God has taken them.' This can make death sound random and imminent; it might leave your child afraid that more of their loved ones, or even themselves, are in constant danger of being taken.

Instead, explain what caused the person's death and how your child can keep themselves safe, and then, if it is part of your belief system, you can tell them about an afterlife with God.

AVOID: 'They have gone to sleep.' Particularly for young children, this euphemism can leave them afraid to go to sleep.

Instead, explain in a concrete way what death means—including that we no longer breathe and that our heart stops beating. Your child may be upset at first, but children can cope with the truth better than we often realise.

IMAGE SOURCE WHITE/THINKSTOCK

Use simple, factual language: don't be afraid to use the words 'death' and 'dead'. Children are aware of death from a young age in relation to nature—and so it is much better to be open and frank with them, rather than confusing them with misleading (although seemingly comforting) euphemisms.

Grieving

Throughout the grieving process, your child will continue to need information. Be willing to answer their questions, and help them explore their theories about death, afterlife and related issues. Get them involved in planning for the funeral or memorial, which can be a great outlet to express their love for the person who has died—as long as they know what to expect, and feel they have a choice over whether to attend. Don't press them to talk, but you might deliberately find time alone with them (perhaps at bedtime, or in the car) to give them the chance to raise the issue if they would like. More introverted children (see p. 39) may prefer to be given books or films about grieving rather than talking aloud—at least at first. Give them time to process and then come back with more questions.

As far as possible, try to maintain a normal routine; this will reassure your child that their basic needs are still being met. Encourage them to do things they enjoy; reassure them that both grief and happiness are acceptable emotions to feel during this time. Don't take any difficult behaviour personally; enforce boundaries as usual but take care to respond to the emotions causing this behaviour. You want to stay tuned in to how your child is feeling, but avoid asking them constantly or treating them too delicately. All that matters is that whenever your child does want to talk through their emotions, they know that you're there.

Memorialising a loved one

After a death, take care to keep talking about the lost loved one. Deliberately mention their name, and reminisce over memories of them, perhaps creating a memory box or scrapbook. Death is final in many ways, but it doesn't mean that they can't continue to be an important part of your child's life. ∎

THIS MIGHT HELP

There are plenty of books about grieving and loss that can help children understand their emotions. I particularly recommend:

The Next Place by Warren Hanson

Tear Soup by Pat Schwiebert and Chuck DeKlyen

The Invisible String by Patrice Karst

The Fall of Freddie the Leaf by Leo Buscaglia

THIS MIGHT HELP

There are several companies that can help support children dealing with bereavement, such as Winston's Wish or Childhood Bereavement UK.

The companies Together For Short Lives and Rainbow Trust support families with children who have themselves been diagnosed with a life-threatening condition.

Parents

When your family is going through a difficult time, it can be tempting to stifle your own needs in order to look after those of your child. Alternatively, it's easy to retreat inside yourself. What you need is a balance: take care of your own emotional and physical needs, and allow yourself to express your feelings, so that you are strong enough to support your child as well.

JACK HOLLINGSWORTH/DIGITALVISION/THINKSTOCK

FIND A SUPPORT SYSTEM

Your child cannot fulfil all of your emotional needs—and nor should you expect them to. Make sure you have time away from your child with a partner, friend, relative or therapist who can support you. You may feel guilty leaving your child, but it is ultimately much better for them not to be the only person in your life: they will feel and struggle with this pressure.

TAKE CARE OF YOURSELF

While you should remain honest with your child about the range of emotions you are feeling, they do not need to witness your raw pain and anger. Find some time alone or with close friends or relatives, and allow yourself to cry or be angry. Then, you will be better equipped to explain your sadness to your child without frightening them with your emotional distress.

DON'T ABSORB YOUR CHILD'S PAIN

As parents, it is hard not to be sad when our child is sad. If your child has a problem of their own—being bullied, for example—you will no doubt feel devastated on their behalf, but try not to let this overcome you, especially in front of your child. Focus instead on being a parent.

DON'T EXPECT TOO MUCH OF YOURSELF

Set no expectations of your own behaviour. This is hard on you too, and it's OK if you don't react perfectly in every situation. You're bound to get a few things wrong, but you and your child will do just fine. And anyway, you'll make your best decisions when you're not feeling stress about doing the right thing.

ACCEPT YOUR STRESS

You will feel a lot of negative emotions during this difficult time, and it will only hurt you to try to ignore them or repress them. The best thing you can do is accept that you're feeling stressed, sad or angry, and try to work out exactly what is hurting you so that you can address it.

SHOULD I LIMIT HOW MUCH MY CHILD USES TECHNOLOGY?

One of the biggest challenges for parents today is trying to figure out our child's relationship to the digital world.

Technology has forever changed the way that children grow and develop. We know that the brain is highly sensitive to the world in which it exists, and so growing up around technology will literally affect our child's brain. The digital world brings great advantages to the lives of children, but there are still risks—and parents need to be informed about how much use of digital devices is sensible. Remember, children may be naturally tech-savvy, but they still require support and boundaries in the digital world as in any other area of

their life. With a bit of guidance, your child will learn to use technology to support their emotional, mental and physical wellbeing.

The effects of technology

There are many aspects of your child's wellbeing which might be affected by the digital world. From when they are very young, technology can cause a reduction in physical activity. Babies and young children need to be crawling, walking, climbing and generally exploring their physical environments—but a child entertained on an iPad is less likely to move around. Excessive technology use can also be detrimental to a child's

motor and fine skills, which are developed through physical play with tangible objects of different shapes and sizes, and movement through a variety of physical environments.

Your child's communication skills are dependent on them interacting with numerous different people. Reading other people's facial expressions is vital in a child's development of empathy and compassion. If communication takes place too predominantly via technology, this development may be hampered. However, FaceTime or Skype is a great way to keep in touch with distant friends or relatives—so do take advantage of this.

ARTFOLIOPHOTO/ISTOCK/THINKSTOCK

4 TIPS FOR LIMITING TECHNOLOGY USE

1 Make sure the whole family has some **time away from screens** every day—or even whole screen-free days once a week or month.

2 Keep digital devices **away from the table** at meals, as this can interrupt important family time.

3 Digital devices should **stay out of the bedroom at night** (see p. 22 for more on technology and sleep). You might have a charging station downstairs where the whole family leaves their phones overnight. Ideally, the whole family should avoid looking at screens for at least 30 minutes before bedtime.

4 Think about **what your child actually needs** from a digital device at each age. If there is a reason they will need to make calls, start with a simple phone with no Internet access (although no phone until secondary school is ideal). Once they have demonstrated appropriate use, you can decide if they are ready for a smartphone. The same applies to needing a personal laptop: can they use the family computer for now?

Set some ground rules

Excessive use of technology can be as harmful for adults as it can for children, so the whole family should follow some basic ground rules. There will always be other parents who are either stricter or more liberal than you—and a classic complaint from children is that 'all their friends are allowed' to do something they're not. Remember that you have set your family rules in the best interests of your children. Be ready to listen to your child's arguments, and adapt the rules if you think your child has a reasonable point, but do not be swayed by parent-to-parent peer pressure, or a desire to be liked by your children.

Discuss your digital family rules in advance, considering very carefully at what age your child should first have a smartphone, tablet or laptop, and what the usage boundaries need to be. Do the same thing regarding social networks: these websites will be an important part of your child's social life, but look at the age guidelines first, and set some boundaries for how much time your child can spend on these sites.

Some parents and children find it helpful if the agreement is written down in advance. Technology can be addictive and consuming, so it is worth having clear boundaries in place before your child gets their hands on a digital device. Once the genie is out of the bottle, it is difficult to put it back!

Talk to your family and friends about your agreement and ask them to support it: if a grandparent or godparent presents your child with a laptop or tablet as a gift, it can cause serious conflict if you take it away. ◼

> Once your child has a smartphone, they will have 24-hour access to the web, so think carefully about when to take this step. Children do not need a smartphone before secondary school, and even then you might consider limiting their Internet until they are used to managing their use of the phone.

> Screen time for children under two years old should be limited to 15–30 minutes daily: always interactive, and always with a parent. Children aged two to five should be limited to 30 minutes to an hour of screen time a day. Once they hit five, this can be gradually and incrementally increased until they are 11 or 12, when they should be limited to two hours maximum. This limit should include all screens, from televisions to laptops to phones.

SHOULD I
CONTROL
WHAT MY CHILD
LOOKS AT?

The digital world gives children access to a wealth of information, making it both a fantastic resource and a minefield. Technology gives children access to inappropriate material such as pornography, hate speech or pro-eating disorder websites—as well as exposing them to the 24-hour news cycle, which may worry or frighten them.

What we need to accept is that we cannot totally control what our children see. Even if you have parental controls on all your technology at home, your child may well see or hear about inappropriate content from other children at their school—and you shouldn't overreact if they do so: respect that different houses have different rules. While you can certainly try to limit what your child looks at, make it clear to them that they can ask you questions about any age-inappropriate content that they do come across. It is important that we respond to their fears and worries, and help them make sense of what they have seen or heard.

With support and guidance, your child can use the boundless information available to them to gain a wider understanding of their world, an appreciation for what they have ▶

> Children under the age of six can find some images on the news very distressing. At this age, they may struggle to distinguish facts from fantasy, and may believe that what they are watching is happening in real time: this makes repeated viewing of the same event particularly harrowing. They will not be able to distance themselves from what they see: violent footage from a far-off, war-torn country can leave a child worrying that they are in danger.

6 TIPS FOR
WATCHING THE NEWS

AUTHOR'S TIPS

1 It is not necessary for younger children to watch the news live. **Look at the news first**, gauge its suitability, and prepare yourself to answer questions before watching or reading it together with your child.

2 Put **parental controls** on news websites on your child's digital device. You can't shield them entirely, but this will prevent them reading frightening news alone, perhaps at night.

3 Seek out **positive news** to share with your child to balance out the sad or scary stories that dominate TV news, and that their friends are more likely to share with them.

4 **Listen** when your child wants to tell you about news they've come across.

5 **Avoid repeated screenings** of specific incidences: this can leave haunting images in your child's head.

6 Cultivate an **ongoing dialogue** about what is going on in the world. Discuss what you see together, and ask follow-up questions.

AMANAIMAGESRF/THINKSTOCK

in comparison to others, and respect for differing attitudes and experiences.

Monitoring online behaviour

Set ground rules in advance for the online behaviour you will and will not tolerate. It is important that your child doesn't feel their privacy is being invaded (**see p. 47**) by having their device unexpectedly checked; if you do wish to randomly check your child's devices (and this is advisable), then make it clear from the beginning that this will be happening.

24-hour news

Many parents are keen for their children to stay informed and to become intellectually engaged with their world. This is a positive ideal: the digital world means that children today are growing up in a global community (**see p. 34**). However, there is a health warning required: we now have a 24-hour constant stream of news—on our own TVs, radios, tablets and smartphones but also in the background of shops, cafés, even doctors' waiting rooms—and this overload of information can be harmful. Parents should monitor their child's access to this constant stream of information—and indeed their own.

The news today is extraordinarily fast-paced: investigative journalism is becoming a thing of the past. The vast proportion of news today is negative and knee-jerk, often led by Twitter, and in many cases not even accurate. Rarely do we go back and revisit past news to update ourselves on the outcome: the news is now saturated with soundbites rather than quests for truth.

Bad news sells—but an overload of negative information is certainly not helpful to a child's wellbeing. This has been backed up my a multitude of research; as far back as 1997, the British Journal of Psychology published a research paper on the psychologic impact of negative TV news bulletins — and this has only become worse as the news has spread to our computers, tablets and smartphones.

You can't shield your child from this news, but you can restrict their access to it, and reduce the amount of time they spend being bombarded with it. Digital media is here to stay—and it contributes a lot to our world—but it requires wisdom to navigate.

Background television or radio

Many of us today have the television or radio constantly on in the background, much like in the past we would have music. This may seem harmless, but in excess it can be detrimental for the whole family—particularly for children.

Not only is it distracting and unhelpful for relaxing, background television can expose children to disturbing content out of context. Many of us tune out the sound of the television as we go about our days, but a child may absorb misleading snippets of information which, when unexplained, can leave them confused and frightened. ∎

JUPITERIMAGES/PIXLAND/THINKSTOCK

TRY PHRASING IT THIS WAY

AVOID: 'Why are you worried?' This can come across as an accusatory question—and besides, young children are not always sure exactly why they are worried.

Instead, try: 'What have you heard?' or 'How is it making you feel?' If a young child is having nightmares, ask them to describe the dream and identify the key emotions.

THIS MIGHT HELP

The website and magazine **Positive News** is filled with uplifting news stories. You may wish to share some of these with your child.

First News or **The Week** for children are great resources to introduce your child to what's going on in the world.

Parents

The digital world is no longer just for those born this side of the millennium. Increasingly, much of adults' lives are taking place online as well: our jobs, our newspapers, our books, our friends. With our phones constantly buzzing, it can be hard to relax and enjoy time with our children—but if we don't find a way to switch off, it can be damaging to our own mental health as well.

THINKSTOCK

TAKE NOTE OF WHAT YOU CAN HANDLE

Some content online or in the news can be terribly upsetting even for adults. While you may feel under pressure to stay informed, be gentle with yourself when dealing with troubling news stories, particularly if you are feeling stressed or fragile. There's a reason that news channels warn you of upcoming sensitive content: it's OK if you decide you're not feeling strong enough to face it right away.

ASK YOURSELF...

What am I modelling to my children in relation to my use of digital devices?

ASK YOURSELF...

Do I ever use my phone while talking to my children?

SWITCH OFF AT NIGHT

It's not just the children who need some time away from screen at night time; you'll sleep much better if you can power down your own phone and laptop for at least an hour before your head hits the pillow.

TURN OFF NOTIFICATIONS

As a parent, it's easy to feel like you need your phone on at all times in case of emergencies. When your child is out of the house, every noise your phone makes can illicit a panic response. To make for a calmer environment, most smartphones will let you turn off all but the most important notifications. For example, you could set it so that your child's number (if they have a phone) or the number of whoever is looking after them will get through, but everything else is muted, leaving you to relax and read your book in peace.

WHAT IS MINDFULNESS?

MONKEYBUSINESSIMAGES/ISTOCK/THINKSTOCK

Thanks to a flurry of books, apps and courses, mindfulness has become the buzzword of the moment—leading to a lot of misunderstandings about what it actually is, and at times, a total misrepresentation of it in the media. There are some extremely helpful books and resources out there—but remember, mindfulness is, at its core, about your experience. Reading about it will only get you so far; then you have to live it.

In essence, mindfulness means bringing awareness to our everyday lives. In our busy, fast-moving world, many of us rush around without ever

IN THE KNOW

"Mindfulness is knowing what you are experiencing while you are experiencing it."
GUY ARMSTRONG,
MEDITATION TEACHER

being fully present in our moment-to-moment experiences—and therefore we miss out on much of the rich tapestry of our lives. When we are being mindful, we notice the details of each moment, being open to each thought, feeling or bodily experience, without judging them, reacting to them, or trying to change them. Mindfulness can make people feel more connected to their lives, avoiding the sensation that life is passing one by. There are also health

benefits: lower stress levels, improved sleep, better management of chronic pain, less emotional reactivity.

When trying to be mindful, your mind and attention may well wander off. When you notice this, don't give up; gently and patiently guide the attention back to your present moment. Every time you bring the mind back to the present, you are strengthening your ability to pay attention.

Children are naturally far more mindful than adults, but they lose this as they grow older, and our modern society is threatening to take that away from them at an ever younger age.

The two modes of mind

In the 21st century western world, we have cultivated a one-dimensional relationship with our minds: valuing only the thinking, rational mind. The thinking mind is responsible for reasoning, decision-making, goal-setting, processing and comparing; humans using their minds in this way have advanced the world in wonderful ways.

However, the mind has another mode, and it's just as important: the sensing mind. This mode of mind is about awareness: tasting, hearing, smelling, touching, feeling and experiencing in the moment. In order to function effectively, we need to utilise and cultivate both modes of mind.

The thinking mind is focused on doing. Using our minds in this way allows us to look to the past and future, understand the bigger picture, plan, and make rational decisions. The sensing mind, which we activate using mindfulness, is focused on being. Using our minds this way allows us to look to the present, connect with our bodies, and find a much healthier and more constructive approach to our lives—the good times and the challenging times. ▶

AUTHOR'S TIPS

3 WAYS TO INTRODUCE MINDFULNESS

1 Help your child to **take notice** of what is happening in a specific moment, noticing and savouring each experience.

2 Teach your child to recognise that their **emotions will come and go** rather like clouds: help them accept and experience each one without becoming overwhelmed by it.

3 When your child is stressed or worried, tell them to place one hand on their tummy and one on their chest, close their eyes, and **notice their breathing** for at least ten breaths. Visual children can think of themselves as a snow globe: when it's all shaken up, it's hard to see the picture inside the globe, and no amount of shaking will clear the snow; if they stop shaking it and allow the snow to settle, everything will become clearer.

Mind and body

Despite what the name might suggest, mindfulness is not about delving deeper into our minds: that's actually what we do by default. In his short story 'A Painful Case', James Joyce wrote that one of his characters, Mr Duffy, "lived a short distance from his body". This is a fantastic description that applies to many of us: we spend most of our time inside our own heads, disconnected from our own physical feelings and our five senses.

Children have a naturally greater connection between their mind and body: watch any child jump in a puddle of water and see how much they are enjoying the stamping of their feet, and the sensations of the water splashing on their body.

Children notice the messages their bodies give them moment by moment: from hunger to joy or sadness. They are naturally living in the present moment, but as they grow and develop in our fast-paced world, they lose this precious gift.

Mindfulness can prevent this loss: practising it will enable your child to remain better connected to their body, and to continue picking up on the many messages their body is attempting to send them.

This can help them eat better, recognising when they are full or when the food they are eating is not giving them enough energy (see p. 97 for a mindful eating exercise the family can try together). It can also help them sleep better by relaxing into the sensation of feeling tired; it can inspire them to enjoy exercise as they notice the positive effects of the endorphins.

When your child is struggling with difficult thoughts and feelings, one of the best things you can teach them to do is to move their attention to the physical sensations of their body— perhaps simply the rhythm of their breathing. Not only will this help calm them down, it might also reveal a source of the problem: perhaps your child is feeling upset purely because they are hungry, or have not had enough sleep! It is amazing how strongly connected our physical and mental states can be. Using mindfulness to help your child stay connected to their body will enable them to pick up on this—and be better able to look after themselves.

That's not to say that your child should never use the thinking mode of their mind: thoughts need to be recognised, respected and, when appropriate, acted upon. What is vital is that your child can recognise when they are ruminating or over thinking, and that they understand this is unhelpful. Mindfulness can help your child acknowledge their thoughts while still remaining present in their body. ■

"When our daughter was younger, she hated it when we left the room after saying goodnight, but since using mindfulness at night, that is no longer a problem. She does breathing exercises, then tunes into her body, noticing the feeling of being relaxed. After this, she is happy and settled and ready for sleep."

CLARE, MOTHER OF A SIX-YEAR-OLD

HOW CAN MINDFULNESS HELP MY CHILD MAKE CHOICES?

MONKEYBUSINESSIMAGES/ISTOCK/THINKSTOCK

Many children struggle with indecision; others make quick and uninformed choices that you may worry are not beneficial to them. Practising mindfulness can help your child check in with themselves, and make intentional choices that actually reflect their needs.

Habit vs intention

The human brain is able to function much of the time on autopilot. This means that we can carry out thousands of daily activities without much thought or effort: a huge advantage in our complex and busy world. The problem is that we have ceded too much of our lives to autopilot, meaning we are not fully conscious or present in many experiences which could enrich our lives.

But it's not just the most fulfilling experiences in which our minds and bodies should be focused and engaged. Much of the time, we barely notice what we are doing as we carry out our daily routine—meaning we are not approaching these tasks with intention or choice. (Have you ever noticed that you're driving to the wrong destination in the car, for example?)

Children naturally live in the present moment: an extraordinary gift which is gradually stolen from them by deadlines, homework, and our own need to rush them frantically from one place to another.

Practising mindfulness will help your child maintain their ability to live in the present. When a child is being mindful, they access a higher level of self-awareness and are able to be more intentional with their choices. ■

> Deliberately making the choice to try something new can help your child start being more mindful. For example, they might choose to sit in a different chair than usual, and see how differently the world looks from there. While they're noticing so many new things, they are not acting on autopilot.

HOW CAN MINDFULNESS HELP MY CHILD WITH THEIR WORRIES?

Without mindfulness, much of our time is spent ruminating over a past event, or catastrophising about the future. This mental time-travel can only be beneficial to a certain extent: reflecting on past events can help us learn from them, and making plans for the future can help us make important decisions. Beyond that, time spent worrying can be mentally exhausting.

If your child is worrying about something, help them notice that they are caught up in this worry, and then guide their attention to their breath. This will move them away from the thinking mode and into the sensing mode, allowing the mind to calm. You can then use your thinking minds to come up with a strategy together—and once you have thought through some solutions, return to mindfulness. Left to ruminate, worries can become all-

consuming, and might keep your child up at night. Mindfulness can help your child stay present, and stop agonising over the troubles of their day, or their fears for tomorrow.

Our mind tells us stories

The mind is constantly trying to make sense of the events in our lives and to understand what is happening. This is where our thoughts come from—but they are often based on very little

"A human mind is a wandering mind, and a wandering mind is an unhappy mind. The ability to think about what is not happening is a cognitive achievement that comes at an emotional cost."
MATTHEW KILLINGSWORTH AND DANIEL GILBERT, PSYCHOLOGISTS AT HARVARD UNIVERSITY

evidence.

Imagine the following situation: You are standing at the school gates, and notice some parents looking towards you. You smile and wave, but they do not smile back; in fact, they seem to blank you, and continue talking to each other.

What did you notice as you read through this scenario? Did you find yourself worrying that you had said or done something to offend the other parents, or that they were talking about you or your child? Did you imagine yourself feeling embarrassed, angry or vulnerable?

Now imagine that it turned out the other parents were in fact planning you a surprise party. This beautifully demonstrates how our minds compulsively interpret situations, fill in the gaps and tell us stories that can be totally untrue. Our thoughts are often based on assumptions, or influenced by past experiences; they are not facts, and shouldn't be treated as such. There is a wonderful anonymous quote which describes this perfectly: "I've had a lot of worries in my life—most of which never happened."

Your child's mind can tell them similarly unhelpful stories. They might have a bad day and end up telling themselves they are useless or unpopular—and believing it.

Mindfulness offers a more liberating and constructive way of relating to our thoughts. Through mindfulness, we learn that our thoughts are just thoughts: they offer a running commentary on life, which at times might be useful, but is not always true. Thoughts do not define us either: they are merely events within our mind.

When you explain this to your child, they no longer need to focus on and obsess over every thought. Once they realise they have made assumptions and filled in the gaps, they can accept that there are some things they don't know—and that there is no point worrying about something that may not even be the case. ■

In 2010, researchers at Harvard developed an app to track the happiness of 2,250 individuals. At random times of day, participants received a phone notification asking them how happy they were, what they were doing, and whether they were thinking about their current activity or about something else. Results showed that participants' happiness was largely unrelated to the specific activity they were doing; instead, it was those more engaged in their current activity, whatever that was, who felt the happiest. Sadly, 47% of people at any one time are not engaged with their current activity.

MONKEYBUSINESSIMAGES/ISTOCK/THINKSTOCK

practised mindfulness will be better able to experience an upsetting or irritating event without an instant reaction.

Mindfulness and anger

Without practising mindfulness, we have a tendency to make assumptions, and to believe our every thought. This can leave us in a spiral of anger: we think angrily about why someone might have behaved in a certain way, and these thoughts can become very repetitive.

An angry child may well be telling themselves a story: if, for example, a teacher punished them for something they did not do, they may believe that the teacher is out to get them, and be reacting angrily to that. Using mindfulness, you can help your child realise that they don't actually know the truth, and that it is unhelpful to dwell on their thoughts about the situation. Instead, they can use mindfulness to ground them in the present moment, in which the teacher and the punishment are no longer affecting them. Then, they are better able to come up with a considered response: the next day at school, they can explain to the teacher what really happened. ■

GEORGE MURESAN/ISTOCK/THINKSTOCK

HOW CAN MINDFULNESS HELP MY CHILD MANAGE THEIR EMOTIONS?

Mindfulness helps us respond to situations rather than react to them, which can be key for children prone to difficult behaviour. The human ability to react is crucial for survival: this is what protects us if we have touched something hot, or find ourselves in the path of a car. However, it's not so helpful when we react strongly to remarks made by friends and family which have upset us.

When we are on autopilot, which is how we spend a considerable percentage of our lives, we are more likely to react to any given event with little or no conscious thought. This is what can cause us to shout at our loved ones, or storm away, without waiting to take possession of all the facts. Our reactions are often strongly influenced by tiredness, stress or hunger—but because we are on autopilot, and not connected to our bodies, we don't pick up on this.

Mindfulness enables a more considered response, and leaves room for compassion. A child who has

In 2010, Kimberly Schonert-Reichl and Molly Stewart Lawlor investigated the effects of mindfulness teaching in schools on the behaviour of the pupils. They discovered that the pupils self-reported significantly higher levels of optimism and other positive emotions when they had practised mindfulness three times daily. Teacher reports showed an improvement in the pupils' social competence, and a decrease in aggression and confrontational behaviour.

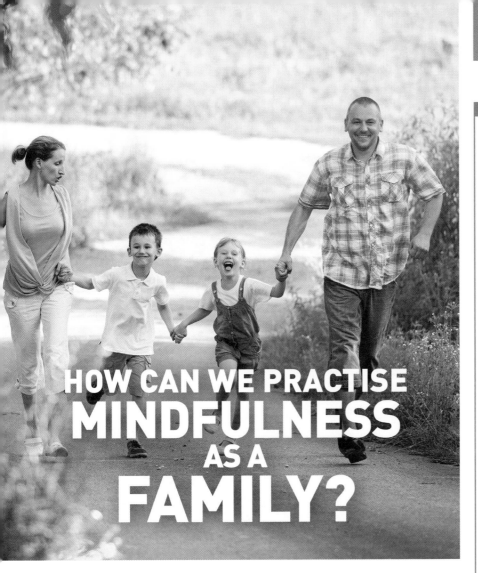

HOW CAN WE PRACTISE MINDFULNESS AS A FAMILY?

AUTHOR'S TIPS

4 MINDFUL PRACTICES FOR THE FAMILY

1 Try **mindful eating**. Take time over meals together, talking about the food, flavours and aromas. Keep this to the first mouthful unless the children are enthusiastic. Alternatively, try eating in silence!

2 Have a **mindful space** within the home, where anyone from the family can go for a moment alone when they are upset, angry or just feel like some time out.

3 Take a **mindful moment at bedtime**, perhaps after a bedtime story. You and your child together should take a few moments to be still, resting your hands on your chest and focusing on your breath as it comes into and leaves the body.

4 Go for a **mindful walk** as a family. Spend five minutes walking in silence, noticing the experience of your body moving and paying attention to the smell, sights, sounds and sensations. See what it feels like walking as quietly as possible, or changing the pace. At the end, talk about what you noticed and felt.

There are numerous ways we can bring mindfulness into our family lives. Mindfulness is multifaceted: it can be practised through formal meditation, but it can also be brought into everyday life.

The essence of mindfulness is about experiencing the present moment without censoring or judging any of the feelings that come with it. It's not about controlling your thoughts or emotions: if, during a mindfulness exercise, your child becomes bored or wants to talk about something else, do not push these feelings away. Give your child a choice (see p. 30) about which mindfulness practices they would like to do, or even allow them to create some exercises of their own. This is especially important if you would like to send them to a mindfulness course; a child who has been forced to attend may end up becoming an unfair distraction for the other children who have actively chosen to be there.

Everyday mindfulness

A great way to introduce the concept of mindfulness to your family is to play a mindful eating game. Pick a treat that your child enjoys, such as a chocolate, and give everybody one to eat normally. Then give everybody another, but this time, you're all just going to look at them as if you'd never seen one before. Notice the colour, shadows, indents, and the weight of them in your hand. With your eyes closed, what do they smell like? What's happening in your mouths: are you salivating? What are you thinking? (Even if it's just 'Get on with it'—that counts!)

Place the treats in your mouths, ▶

but don't bite. Notice the flavour and texture; are they melting? Finally, bite into them. Notice the taste, and your own desire to chew or swallow (without controlling or overpowering this desire).

Don't talk about your thoughts during the exercise; merely savour the experience. When the treat has completely gone, share with each other how different the experience was from the first time. You may find that you enjoyed it more. You may feel full and no longer want to eat another.

This practice shows how much you can miss from your lives when you're functioning on autopilot. The point of the exercise is not just about eating mindfully, although paying attention to what you eat is important in itself (**see p. 92**); it's about being present, and savouring the positive moments throughout your daily life. ∎

THIS MIGHT HELP

Sitting Still Like a Frog by Eline Snel is a book and accompanying CD which offers up mindfulness exercises and practices for parents to try with their children.

"I started listening to the **Sitting Still Like a Frog** CD in the car with my children on the way to school. Principally, I wanted to see the effects on my son, who is often fractious and irritated in the mornings. At first he resisted it, but I found that the exercises calmed him; when we arrive at school, he is a different boy!"

MARTHA, MOTHER OF THREE CHILDREN

THIS MIGHT HELP

Find a course that you can attend as a family. My husband and I run a mindfulness course called Pathways, designed for children and parents or carers. We run the courses within schools, or privately in your home.

Parents

Mindfulness isn't just a resource for your child: it can be invaluable in helping you manage the challenges of being a parent. Using mindfulness, you can develop better relationships with friends, family or a partner— as well as becoming better equipped to approach the tasks of each day.

DON'T WORRY ABOUT TIME

One of the main reasons many people resist mindfulness practice is that they feel they do not have the time. Ironically, research shows that being mindful can actually create more time in our lives: it makes us more productive and aware of each moment, meaning that we can get more done in a day.

ASK YOURSELF...

Do I have a tendency to rush to places even if I'm not in a hurry? Do I pay attention to my experiences while I'm on my way to a destination?

ASK YOURSELF...

How does my child see me react to unexpected or irritating situations?

LET YOUR CHILD LEAD THE WAY

Mindfulness is a gift that comes to children more naturally. To live more mindfully yourself, notice how your child treats their surroundings, and be careful how you react to them. When they jump in a puddle in their brand new shoes, you may be transported to the past (how much you paid for them) or the future (the work involved in cleaning them)—but remember that your child is enjoying a sensory moment. When they are ambling along, asking constant questions about their surroundings, while you are trying to rush them home to start cooking lunch, consider the wonderful mindfulness practice that you could gain by joining them in their curiousity.

STAY IN THE MOMENT

Your existence is rooted in the present moment— and yet we miss so many moments when our minds are caught up in the past or future, or functioning on auto-pilot. The present moment is where you will find sunrises and sunsets, beautiful landscapes, or the feeling of holding your child's hand.

Endorsements

"Wellbeing is surely the heart of what we want for our children. Based on many years of work as a respected psychotherapist and mindfulness teacher with young people, teachers and parents in schools, Julie Johnson offers wonderfully practical and trustworthy guidance on the key questions to ask and how to ensure that we're providing the best possible conditions in our families and schools to help support children and teenagers in developing resilience and wellbeing both now and for the longer-term. Whether your child is flourishing or in crisis, or a mixture of both, there's bite-sized compassionate wisdom here that could be very helpful."

Chris Cullen, psychotherapist and founder of the Mindfulness in Schools Project

"Nowadays, there is intense focus on child and adolescent mental health and wellbeing, and for good reason. Surveys of young people increasingly describe and report increasing levels of mental distress and an ever-increasing range of complex personal and emotional challenges for young people, which if not handled appropriately, can have serious, and in some cases, devastating consequences. Yet many young people do not have ready access to the guidance they need to navigate their way through or around certain personal challenges, and efforts at preventing mental distress and ill health in the first instance are in some cases altogether lacking.

"Wellbeing is a term and concept much heard about these days, but its meanings and uses aren't always clear. Julie Johnson is a recognised expert in this field and the ideas and concepts she describes in this book will help both young people and their parents to understand what wellbeing is and how best to develop it at different stages of a young person's life, and into adulthood. The book is filled with a host of very practical ideas, suggestions and exercises that anyone can apply. This book should become part of the national curriculum as it offers guidance in so many important and sensitive areas rarely taught in schools, and yet wellbeing can have enduring effects throughout one's life. This book conveys the message that wellbeing doesn't simply 'happen' and that we need to plan and work towards it. This book is the ideal 'road map' to take on the journey."

Professor Robert Bor, psychologist and family therapist

"Research shows that wellbeing rather than economic success is critical for the development of happy, healthy and thriving societies. This timely book on children's wellbeing by Julie Johnson offers parents a wise and heartfelt companion to help their family thrive and flourish. In order to foster wellbeing in children, we require an understanding of all our children's needs and their changing nature throughout development. The author illustrates how wellbeing can be implemented on every level of need: physical, emotional, social and existential. The author invites the reader to empathise with both child and parent alike. Realistic case examples help to illustrate the challenges and encourage the reader to try out easy adaptations. Well-validated developmental theories are applied to contemporary challenges of parenting, such how to motivate your child without fostering perfectionistic striving; how to instil self-regulation in relation to the use of digital media and how to foster a sense of responsibility and compassion for others at an age of helicopter parenting. The author translates her wealth of experience as a psychotherapist and pioneering mindfulness teacher for children into kind, wise and highly practical advice that will surely make every parent feel supported."

Dr. Christine Brähler (DClinPsy, PhD), Clinical Psychologist, Psychologische Psychotherapeutin, Supervisor, MSC Teacher Trainer, International Coordinator CMSC (MSC – mindfulness self compassion)

"If you are a parent who wishes to have a better understanding of what children need in order to become their best, then this book is for you. Julie Johnson's book is insightful, well-researched and based on years of experience of working with children and families. It combines new psychological understandings about how to help children become more emotionally resilient with practical ideas and tips any parent can put into practice to make a positive difference to their child's emotional development, academic success and to family life."

Miriam Chachamu, psychotherapist and family therapist

INDEX